Palgrave Macmillan Asian Business Series

Series Editor
Yingqi Wei, Business School
University of Leeds
Leeds, UK

The Palgrave Macmillan Asian Business Series publishes theoretical and empirical studies that contribute forward-looking social perspectives on the study of management issues not just in Asia, but by implication elsewhere. The series specifically aims at the development of new frontiers in the scope, themes and methods of business and management studies in Asia, a region which is seen as key to studies of modern management, organization, strategies, human resources and technologies. The series invites practitioners, policy-makers and academic researchers to join us at the cutting edge of constructive perspectives on Asian management, seeking to contribute towards the development of civil societies in Asia and further a field.

Each submission is submitted for single blind peer review. For further information please see our website: https://www.palgrave.com/gp/book-authors/your-career/early-career-researcher-hub/peer-review-process.

To submit a book proposal for inclusion in this series please email Liz Barlow at: liz.barlow@palgrave.com. Details of how to download a proposal form can be found here: https://www.palgrave.com/gp/book-authors/publishing-guidelines/submit-a-proposal.

This series is indexed in Scopus

Dominique Jolly

The New Threat

China's Rapid Technological Transformation

Dominique Jolly
Independent Advisor
Magagnosc, France

ISSN 2661-8435　　　　　ISSN 2661-8443　(electronic)
Palgrave Macmillan Asian Business Series
ISBN 978-3-031-08689-2　　　ISBN 978-3-031-08690-8　(eBook)
https://doi.org/10.1007/978-3-031-08690-8

© The Author(s), under exclusive licence to Springer Nature Switzerland AG 2022
This work is subject to copyright. All rights are solely and exclusively licensed by the Publisher, whether the whole or part of the material is concerned, specifically the rights of translation, reprinting, reuse of illustrations, recitation, broadcasting, reproduction on microfilms or in any other physical way, and transmission or information storage and retrieval, electronic adaptation, computer software, or by similar or dissimilar methodology now known or hereafter developed.
The use of general descriptive names, registered names, trademarks, service marks, etc. in this publication does not imply, even in the absence of a specific statement, that such names are exempt from the relevant protective laws and regulations and therefore free for general use.
The publisher, the authors, and the editors are safe to assume that the advice and information in this book are believed to be true and accurate at the date of publication. Neither the publisher nor the authors or the editors give a warranty, expressed or implied, with respect to the material contained herein or for any errors or omissions that may have been made. The publisher remains neutral with regard to jurisdictional claims in published maps and institutional affiliations.

This Palgrave Macmillan imprint is published by the registered company Springer Nature Switzerland AG.
The registered company address is: Gewerbestrasse 11, 6330 Cham, Switzerland

To my wife Martine and my children Maxime and Camille.

About the Author

Dominique Jolly (Dominique.R.Jolly@Gmail.com) is an independent advisor on foreign business with China. He works as a consultant for several large companies. He also advises international organizations and foreign governments in the areas of innovation and technology. His assignments have taken him to over 20 countries in Europe, Asia, North America, South America, and Africa. He was previously Professor of Business Strategy. He worked for Webster University Geneva (Switzerland), SKEMA Business School (Sophia-Antipolis, France), the Center on China Innovation at CEIBS (Shanghai, China), HEC Montréal (Montréal, Canada), and Grenoble Ecole de Management (Grenoble, France).

Contents

1 Introduction 1

2 The China Public Policy for Technology Creation 7

3 The Chinese National System of Innovation 29

4 The Iconic Case of Telecommunications 59

5 Companies of the Chinese Internet: The Only Potential Rival to Silicon Valley 75

6 Applications in Other Industries: From Technological Catch-up to International Development 97

7 Applications of the Future 111

8 Seven Challenges 127

9 The Conductor and Its Disciplined Performers 147

Index 151

List of Figures

Fig. 1.1	China bundled all the required components of a national system of innovation	4
Fig. 2.1	Exogamy: a potential for learning from and with the partner	11
Fig. 2.2	Each partner targets resources brought in by the other in the JV	12
Fig. 2.3	Annual outflow of foreign direct investment (FDI) from China between 1982 and 2020. (Source: World Bank)	16
Fig. 3.1	Investments in universities	34
Fig. 3.2	Gross domestic spending on R&D. (Source: OECD)	46
Fig. 3.3	Drivers for foreign R&D centers in China have changed	50
Fig. 3.4	Cost-driven R&D: end of development	51
Fig. 3.5	Marketing-driven R&D: focus on development	52
Fig. 3.6	Knowledge-driven R&D: the full R&D spectrum	53
Fig. 3.7	The Chinese government as a conductor and its performers for technology creation	56
Fig. 4.1	China's telecommunication industry	60
Fig. 4.2	Huawei revenue from 2012 to 2020, by geographical region	61
Fig. 5.1	Number of Internet users in China (from 2008 to 2020)	78
Fig. 5.2	The core business of Alibaba	81
Fig. 6.1	Robot density in the manufacturing industry 2020	108
Fig. 7.1	Sales of plug-in electric passenger cars	115
Fig. 8.1	The switch from cost to innovation	136

List of Tables

Table 2.1	Increasingly sophisticated means to foster technological innovation	8
Table 2.2	Partners of Sino-foreign JVs pool differentiated assets into the cooperation	11
Table 2.3	Science and engineering articles in all fields (1996–2018)	25
Table 2.4	Total patent applications (direct and PCT national phase entries)	26
Table 3.1	China in the PISA rankings (2012–2018)	31
Table 3.2	Number of students registered for the Gaokao (in million)	32
Table 3.3	Higher education in China: number of students enrolled	33
Table 3.4	Higher education in China: number of students graduating per year	33
Table 3.5	Top 20 Chinese universities	35
Table 3.6	Number of researchers per 1000 inhabitants	49
Table 3.7	Chinese regulation framework	55
Table 4.1	Smartphones sold per year worldwide (in million)	66
Table 5.1	Largest Chinese companies by market capitalizations (end of 2021)	76
Table 5.2	Profiles of the Chinese BATX (end of 2021)	77
Table 5.3	Comparing BATX business portfolios	95
Table 6.1	Overview of the industries analyzed in Chap. 6	98
Table 8.1	Top nine startups in China	132

1

Introduction

Abstract China had a glorious period of inventiveness in the ancient times. Yet, it was technologically underdeveloped in its recent history. It is only a few decades since the country put emphasis on technological innovation. This first chapter is an introduction to the different issues covered inside this book: stages of technological development, components of the national system of innovation, focus on leading industries, and the future of technology creation in China.

Keywords Public policy • National system of innovation • Leading industries • Future developments • Future challenges

Many Americans still have an outdated vision of China. Eric Schmidt (2020), former CEO of Google.

If we go back to history, China appears as an innovative country. It is known for major constructions such as the Great Wall and the Grand Canal. The country is also known to be the source of several inventions that have marked the world. These include paper and blast furnaces (fifth century BCE), the compass (fourth century BCE), gunpowder (circa

850), the axial rudder, and the woodcut (the ancestor of printing). During the Warring States era (fifth century BC to 221 BC), the rest of the world sought to grasp the silk-making secret held by the Han. At that time, technology transfers took place from the East to the West. Travelers like Marco Polo (1254–1324) helped to build links.

After this glorious period, a long parenthesis opened. Imperial China was ruled by scholars, an educational aristocracy that emphasized literature and philosophy, and was much less adept in the physical and natural sciences. This political organization impeded technology creation. The industrial revolution did not happen in China. And civil wars, international concessions, collapse of the emperor, all contributed to the economic, scientific, and technological decline of the country.

In 1949, when Mao Zedong created the People's Republic of China (PRC), science and technology were not the priority. Except in very few domains, like the space industry, China was a low-tech country. In 1965, Zhou Enlai (the Prime Minister of the PRC) made sciences and techniques one of the four modernization pillars. Unfortunately, the Great Leap Forward (1958–1961) and the Cultural Revolution (1966–1976) impeded any change and even impacted negatively on the development of sciences and techniques. Consequently, the gap with developed countries at the end of the 1970s was huge.

The Open Door Policy of 1978 decided by Deng Xiaoping was the starting point for a big change: China used knowledge brought by foreign companies to upgrade its non-competitive economy, characterized at that time by poor infrastructures, archaic production tools, obsolete technologies, and old products. International technology transfers were key in this technological upgrade (Fu, 2015). Yet internal efforts were extremely limited: even 20 years after the Open Door Policy, China devoted a small 0.5% of its meager GDP to research and development (see vignette on R&D), while the USA devoted 2.5% and Japan 3% (source: OECD).

> **Vignette: What Do We Mean by R&D?**
> Research can be split into fundamental (or basic) research and applied research (OECD, 2015). The outputs of the first one are scientific papers and patents, while the second produces patents and prototypes. Fundamental research is mostly conducted in universities and public research centers, and rarely in companies. Applied research is commonly conducted in companies. Development can also be split into two steps: primary development and end of development. Primary development produces patents, while end of development results in products and processes. End of development is connected with production units. According to OECD, most of the cost (65% on average) is incurred in development. Applied research is second in the budget (25%), and fundamental research the lowest budget (10%).

This book is about modern China. It was written with the willingness to cast a light on a situation which is badly understood and even sometimes unknown in the West. Many foreigners still ignore the recent accomplishments made by China in the field of technology creation. Many think that China is still stuck in duplicating western technologies at a lower cost. They do not see China capable of accomplishing true innovations. Yet, the technological landscape has changed considerably since the beginning of 2000 (Haour & Jolly, 2014; Fu, 2015). China now exhibits some significant companies in high-tech sectors such as telecommunications, the Internet, high-speed train, and the nuclear industry. How have these tech companies, which started from scratch in a so-called socialist market economy, been able to accomplish such an impressive growth (in revenue, staff, patents, market value, etc.)? As a complement to previous work like the one of Mathews (2006), which explained the global success of latecomer firms from the periphery (South Korea, Singapore, Taiwan, Hong Kong, Indonesia, etc.) by their organizational innovations, this book puts the emphasis on technological innovation. The ambition of this book is precisely to cast a light on this dimension.

The aim of the book is to bring out different situations, that is, industries where China already established a leadership, industries where the country has serious options for the future, and industries for which the country will have difficulties to do better than the West. A very special emphasis is put on the role of Chinese authorities as the supreme conductor, and the role devoted to companies (public, but also private and foreign) which have to act as disciplined performers and will stay in the game if they keep themselves aligned with the rules written by the state.

Academics will find in this book a model of the stages through which the country achieved technology creation; this model is used to depict the degree of development of several industries. Academics will also find developments on the concept of national system of innovation. The book clarifies the ingredients needed for a country to enter into technology creation—and applies this framework to grasp the Chinese case with the appropriate data and illustrations. And business people will find the description of successful strategies conducted by Chinese companies in different industries and understand the reasons for their success. They will also find explanations of the stakes regarding the future of China in technology creation and the challenges that will have to be overcome. Let's expose the content of the book.

Chapter 2 offers a four-stage development model starting with the Open Door Policy, supported by several policies which helped the country to climb the technological ladder. Since then, China has been able to gather all the necessary ingredients to produce technological innovation. Figure 1.1 gives an overall picture. Those seven essential components will be listed in Chap. 3.

Fig. 1.1 China bundled all the required components of a national system of innovation

Things have changed dramatically for Chinese companies but also for foreign companies. They cannot recycle their old technologies in China anymore; this is a strategy of the past. Chapter 3 will also look at what they can do today.

After devoting Chap. 3 to the macro perspective, the following three chapters focus on the micro level by analyzing several companies' case studies. The next three chapters look in depth at technological strategies and competitive moves in different industries. Telecommunications, with the leading companies Huawei, Xiaomi, and China Mobile, are an iconic case considering the success of Huawei and Xiaomi not only in China, but also outside China; this case is developed in Chap. 4. One of the lessons learned from this industry is the role played by foreign companies in bringing the initial knowledge base followed by significant domestic investment in R&D by Chinese companies to nurture this base. A second lesson is the benefit which can be gained from a massive market which amplified scale effects at all stages of the value chain. Finally, this industry demonstrates the role the government plays in protecting its national champions.

The Internet is one domain where China has been the fertile ground for the expansion of several national champions—including the famous BAT trio: Baidu, Alibaba, and Tencent. The strategies of those big three and some other smaller players are analyzed in Chap. 5. The chapter highlights some common features such as their connection to the authorities, a good match with local demand, their financial backing up from foreign investors, and a strong technology investment. But China's potential goes beyond telecommunications and the Internet. Some other industries—including the high-speed train and the nuclear industry—have caught up with the West; they are analyzed in Chap. 6. Chapters 4, 5, and 6 show that both the private sector and the Chinese State-Owned Enterprises (SOE) played a role in fostering innovation. Yet, private companies were the overwhelming driving force in industries like the Internet.

Chapter 7 deals with future applications. China has caught up with the West in several areas and is even developing some advanced technologies in the car industry (with the electric and driverless cars), the blockchain, Fintech, and artificial intelligence. Yet, as the ying-yang dialectic teaches us, the sunny side comes with clouds. An overview of seven challenges to overcome is given in Chap. 8.

References

Fu, X. (2015). *China's path to innovation*. Cambridge University Press.
Haour, G., & Jolly, D. (2014). China: The next innovation hot spot for the world. *The Journal of Business Strategy, 35*(1), 2–8.
Mathews, J. (2006). Dragon multinationals: New players in 21st century globalization. *Asia Pacific Journal of Management, 23*(1), 5–27.
OECD. (2015). *Frascati manual 2015: Guidelines for collecting and reporting data on research and experimental development*. The Measurement of Scientific, Technological and Innovation Activities, OECD Publishing. https://doi.org/10.1787/9789264239012-en

2

The China Public Policy for Technology Creation

Abstract The economy of the People's Republic of China has gone through four stages since 1978. At that time, the challenge was to deal with outdated production tools and models. The upgrade took shape with the Sino-foreign joint-ventures; foreign partners were asked to bring new tech to access the Chinese market. The second stage was for Chinese partners to absorb and assimilate this new knowledge. The third stage was to reproduce this knowledge outside the joint-venture thanks to staff moves. In parallel, Chinese authorities started to build the basis of a truly national system of innovation capable of indigenous innovation. The chapter concludes with statistical evidence of progress made both at the inception of the innovation process with the production of scientific articles, and at the end with the number of patent applications.

Keywords Public policy • Upgrading • Sino-foreign joint-venture • Learning • Catch-up • Diaspora

The Chinese government plays a key role in defining the country's strategy for technology creation. Public policy is the driver. That's one demonstration of the compelling power of the State and the Chinese communist party in China. This chapter traces the four phases decided by the Chinese authorities regarding technology creation. China's technology strategy reproduced the trajectory developed by Kim (1997) on South Korea, from learning through imports to indigenous innovation—however, on a much larger scale:

- The first step has been the importation of foreign technologies from advanced countries.[1]
- The next step has been their absorption and assimilation by local companies.
- The following step has been the imitation, that is, to locally reproduce foreign technologies.
- The last step has been to set up the conditions needed for indigenous innovation.

In parallel to steps 1–3, China bundled the resources needed for indigenous innovation. Public policies favored the accumulation of knowledge and capabilities at the level of both individuals and organizations. China does not want to be a follower. That's why this fourth step was to target industries where technological leaps could be envisioned.

Table 2.1 reports the different means preferably used along those four phases. In this table, it appears that those means to foster technological innovation have been increasingly sophisticated.

Timing has differed from one industry to another. The telecom equipment, the Internet companies, and the Fintech went through all the four steps. The high-speed train and the semiconductor industry went through phases 1 and 3. Mass-retailing went as well through the first three steps. The car industry went only through steps 1 and 2; Chinese car manufacturers failed to reproduce quality levels and innovation of Western competitors. And, the pharmaceutical and the construction of jet engines and large aircraft are still in phase 1.

---

[1] Chinese trajectory differs significantly from the Japanese one as Japan has not been very open to foreign investment, while a large part of the Chinese development is due to imports of technologies from advanced countries.

Table 2.1 Increasingly sophisticated means to foster technological innovation

Steps	Importation of foreign technologies	Absorption, assimilation	Reproduction	Indigenous innovation
Means	– Sino-foreign joint-venture – Acquisition of foreign equipment – Licensing agreements – Spying, intellectual property theft	– Training of Chinese staff – Attract diaspora – Hiring of specialist foreigners – Send selected Chinese students abroad	– Constitution of alliance portfolios – Rotation of Chinese personnel – Acquisition of foreign companies – Start local R&D	– Acquisition of foreign high-tech startups – Open innovation – Chinese R&D centers implemented outside China

Those four stages are described in the first three sections of this chapter. Finally, the last section of the chapter shows the recent and impressive achievements made in terms of scientific publications and patent applications. This will raise the question of how this has been possible and will be followed by Chap. 3 and the seven key ingredients needed to forge an efficient national system of innovation.

Chapter 2 relies on research conducted by the author on Sino-foreign joint ventures, learning in joint-ventures, absorption capabilities, and technological catch-up Chinese strategies; the chapter also shows the areas where China is still behind developed countries.

2.1 Learning from Developed Countries in Sino-Foreign JVs

From Maoist Autarky to Deng's Opening

China borrowed a lot. It borrowed Buddhism from India. It borrowed Marxism-Leninism from Russia. The same pattern prevails on economic and technology grounds. During the Mao years (1949–1976), the motto was "Rely on our own strengths"; yet, the country benefited from technical transfers from the Soviets. When Mao died in 1976, China lagged behind in technology in almost all areas. The few Chinese persons who had traveled abroad before 1978 (including Deng Xiaoping) were able to grasp the dramatic underdevelopment of their country. The arrival of Deng Xiaoping in 1978 marks a turning point toward the aspiration for foreign knowledge and the beginning of a policy of sucking up technologies from abroad. His "Open Door Policy" came with the obligation to form joint-ventures between Chinese and foreign companies. Thanks to this wise political posture, Sino-foreign joint-ventures became the main means to learn from the West. At that time, the situation in China is that of a low-tech ocean out of which few highly technical islands were emerging. The goal was to upgrade an industry beyond totally outdated standard. The country's strategy has been to ensure upgrading first in activities with low technical content and then gradually increasing technological sophistication.

Technological Learning Originated from Sino-Foreign Joint-Ventures

Much of the technological learning took place in joint-ventures established with foreign companies. Sino-foreign joint-ventures have an exogamic nature (Jolly, 2005): partners come from unrelated environments (history, values, culture, economics, political, etc.), exhibit unrelated morphological profiles, and each partner brings a different and non-overlapping set of idiosyncratic resources into the joint-venture, as summarized by Table 2.2.

This is because of their exogamic nature that knowledge transfers can occur as depicted by Fig. 2.1. Technologies pumped out of joint-ventures found their way into other companies, 100% Chinese this time, which gradually learned to absorb, assimilate, imitate, and duplicate what they learned from foreigners.

At the company level, two conditions are needed for the assimilation of technologies. The receptor must first develop absorption capacities so that the transfer can take place (Jolly & Thérin, 2007); if there are no staff who can understand it, if there are no means on site to receive the transfer, it will not take shape (Mazloomi Khamseh & Jolly, 2008). Over the years, Chinese staff have learned through contacts with foreign managers

2 The China Public Policy for Technology Creation

Table 2.2 Partners of Sino-foreign JVs pool differentiated assets into the cooperation

Resources brought by Chinese partner	Resources brought by foreign partner
1. Access to physical assets	1. Industrial know-how
2. Access to labor market	2. Product technologies
3. Access to local suppliers	3. Process technologies
4. Access to utilities	4. Manufacturing know-how
5. Access to distribution networks	5. Research equipment
6. *Guan xi* (关系)[a]	6. Managerial skills
	7. Brands
Resources locally rooted and improved when used (except 1).	Resources easy to transfer, but subject to obsolescence (except 6 and 7).

Source: Jolly (2004)
[a]Chinese people prefer to do business with individuals who are familiar to them. A Chinese entrepreneur will use his network of friends to be introduced to potential clients. This intermediation helps to build trust. You have to have "guanxi." In a compact way, guanxi can be defined as "the social capital amassed by an individual." Guanxi is interpersonal. It is not an association, a grouping, a caste, but a sum of connections between individuals

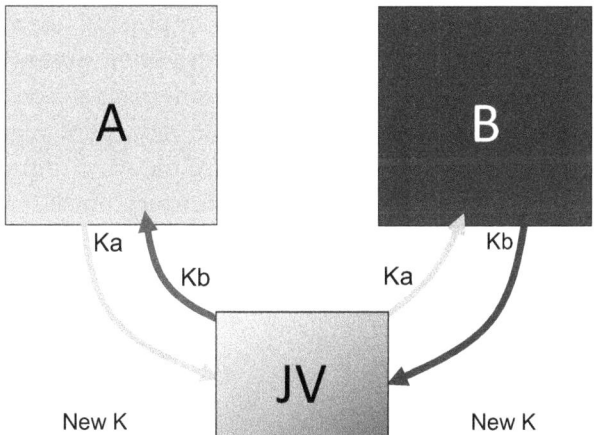

Fig. 2.1 Exogamy: a potential for learning from and with the partner

dispatched to the site by their headquarters. The development of absorption capabilities has been the opportunity for Chinese companies to target appropriate personnel, that is, people capable to understand, receive the transfer, and implement it into a new unit.

The second condition is that it has to be done gradually. Assimilation requires foundations. One country cannot jump immediately into advanced technologies before taking roots in elementary technologies. In China, things were done progressively: most of the first joint-ventures of the 1980s were set up in light industries, that is, in sectors with low technical intensity. Once these foundations are established, a business may consider tackling things a little more complicated. Over the years, there has been a gradual move upmarket. The technological upgrade happened step by step. The move upmarket toward technical products is also a social turning point toward a less servile and more qualified workforce. It will irreparably pose the problem of maintaining full employment.

Foreign Companies Have Also Learned

As illustrated by Fig. 2.2, the learning is not a simple one-way process.

The learning of the Chinese partner is targeting any technological resource brought in by the foreigner. The learning of foreigners is focused on the conditions of establishment: access to physical assets, the labor market, local suppliers, public services, distribution networks—not to mention the construction of guanxi. This means that partners pursue different but symmetrical learning objectives. In those joint-ventures, partners sleep in the same bed, but do not have the same dream. A major consequence is that over a long period, the learning process occurring in

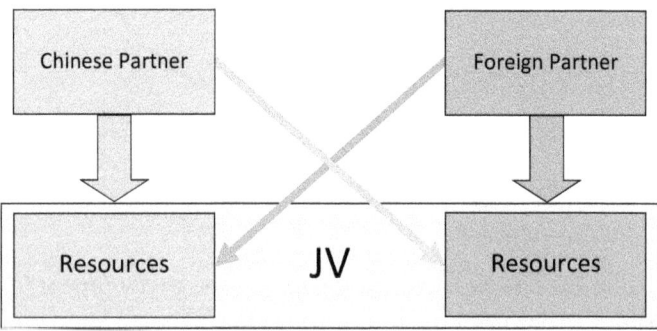

Fig. 2.2 Each partner targets resources brought in by the other in the JV

both ways tends to reduce the idiosyncrasy of partner's profiles. As such, the joint-venture moves from exogamy to endogamy (Jolly, 2006). This transformation explains that most Sino-foreign joint-ventures do not survive over a long period.

Other Means for Learning

The new China started in 1978 by learning from developed countries, notably through Sino-foreign joint-ventures, but also with the acquisition of foreign equipment, licensing contracts, subcontracting, hiring of specialist foreigners and returnees, and the spill-overs from foreign investment.

Spill-overs embody through labor mobility. When Chinese employees move from the joint-venture back to their company of origin, or after having been recruited by a competitor, they come with the knowledge learned in the joint-venture. And, once this knowledge is transferred and demonstrated in a Chinese company, it starts also to be spread into other Chinese companies again thanks to new staff moves. In addition, demonstration effects impact both the competitors of one given business, but also the value chain of the industry backward and forward.

More recently, other means such as venture capital investments and company acquisitions have been used by Chinese firms. In addition, a company that is particularly fond of technological innovations fuels innovation players. There is a strong propensity in the population to test and then adopt new technologies. Payment by mobile phone is an illustration of the almost general adoption of a new technology (see vignette in Chap. 7). The pace of adoption of existing and new technologies has enabled China economy to increase its productivity (and thus partly absorb the increased cost of labor).

We also have to take into account the return of the diaspora and the contingents of Chinese students who studied abroad; China is the biggest provider of foreign students in the world and a very large part of doctoral students in the USA are Chinese (see vignette on the diaspora).

Vignette: The Chinese Diaspora
The Chinese diaspora represents 50 million persons worldwide. This encompasses foreign people with a Chinese origin (like in Malaysia or Singapore)—they are the *huaqiao*. The diaspora also includes Chinese citizens who spent 10 or 20 years abroad first studying at the university and then in the USA (or elsewhere), graduating from an engineering school, and then working for a company like, for example, General Electric—they are called *haigui*. All these people, whether temporarily settled or established abroad for several generations, have key assets—thanks to the knowledge accumulated throughout their stay abroad. This may be technical, commercial, or even legal knowledge and expertise. But, there is also an important skill, namely, the ability to understand and work with foreigners.

The diaspora has made a significant contribution to pulling China out of its isolation. The government targeted (less than 40 years old) engineers and scientists of a Chinese origin and established in leading technological countries (like the USA, or Europe). The return to the country of Chinese nationals is an essential asset. They play an interface role, and they are an accelerator of China's economic development. Chinese private companies and foreign companies hire returnees, in particular for their ability to bridge the gap with foreign countries and to give an international dimension to their activities. These people often have more freedom and support in China to do whatever they want in business than they have in the USA or Europe.

The examples are numerous. For example, Suntech, the former Chinese champion of photovoltaic panels, was founded by Shi Zhengrong who returned home after studying at the University of New South Wales in Australia. In other fields such as pharmaceuticals and biotechnologies, the *haigui* have created most of the startups in China. On the side of scientists, the relative academic freedom that prevails in China can act as a driver. This freedom obviously does not extend to the political sphere; the diaspora returning to China must comply with the fundamental rule: they

(*continued*)

(continued)
must accept the ruling of China by the Chinese communist party (unless the diaspora becomes a hotbed for the emergence of revolutionary forces!). However, these return movements did not slow down the initial inside-out movements. Many Chinese go abroad to try their chance. Their destination is never random but guided by the networks already in place. They frequently establish themselves in the commerce and distribution sectors.

2.2 The Reproduction of Foreign Technologies in Chinese Companies

Alliance Portfolios Built by Chinese Companies

The learning was conducted in many sectors: railway equipment, photovoltaic panels, nuclear power plants, automobile manufacturing, and so forth. Some Chinese firms have developed significant portfolios of alliances, which are all sources of learning. The manufacturer First Automotive Work (FAW) has four partners: General Motors, Volkswagen, Mazda, and Toyota. In the same industry, Chang-An is another example. This automaker has joint-ventures with Mazda, Ford, Suzuki, and PSA. Dongfeng is the most successful example. It is in the middle of a network of joint-ventures with Honda, Nissan, Infiniti, Peugeot–Citroën, Hyundai, and recently Renault, that is, it means to connect with the world's best know-how in the business. Each of these joint-ventures is an opportunity for Chinese manufacturers to observe in situ, over a long period of time, the practices that the foreign partner has imported via the charters of expatriates who came to China. Staff movement from the joint-venture to the unit under full control of the Chinese company helps this one to reproduce what has been observed in the joint-venture.

Learning Through Acquisitions

As shown in Fig. 2.3, since 2005, Chinese outward foreign direct investment (FDI) has grown dramatically. Chinese firms have embarked on the acquisition of companies abroad (much more than green-field investments). Outward FDI picked up in 2016 and came back to more reasonable levels (comparable to inward FDI) in 2020. In their pursuit of international expansion, Chinese companies use these acquisitions as a springboard to acquire abroad strategic resources so to overcome their latecomer disadvantage (Luo & Tung, 2007).

As a recent move, Chinese firms are still relatively inexperienced after less than 20 years. One of the first important deals was the takeover of Volvo by Geely (see vignette). This case has shown that the foreign acquisition can be used to access Western knowledge and simultaneously to give access to the Chinese market to the company acquired.

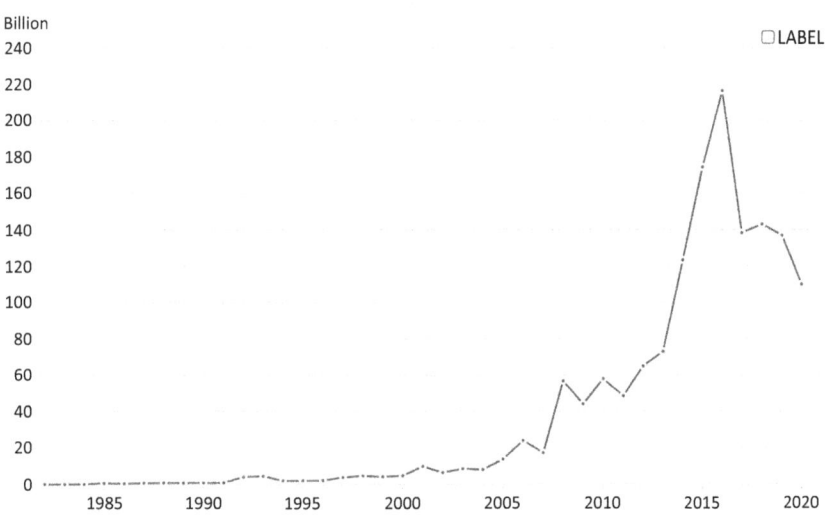

Fig. 2.3 Annual outflow of foreign direct investment (FDI) from China between 1982 and 2020. (Source: World Bank)

Vignette: The Takeover of Volvo by Geely
Geely is a Chinese car manufacturer created in 1998 by Li Shufu (58 years old in 2022) in Hangzhou (Zhejiang). The city is known for its many private businesses (Alibaba being the first one). Li Shufu had previously tried for ten years to launch companies in refrigerators and motorcycles, but unsuccessfully. He entered into the automotive industry by buying a shop that was bankrupt, but which held a license to produce cars. From the creation to 2009, the production went up to 330,000 cars. Geely is listed on the Hong Kong Stock Exchange.

Geely bought the Swedish Volvo Cars from Ford in 2010 for $1.8 billion (1.3 billion euros). This is an operation that opened China to Volvo: three new assembly plants were built in Chengdu, Taizhou (Zhejiang), and Daqing (Heilongjiang) as well as an engine plant (in Zhangjiakou). The attitude adopted by Geely toward Volvo contrasts with the choices made by SAIC when it took over the Korean SsangYong in 2004: SAIC did not understand how South Korean workers operate and furthermore, it tried to bring SsangYong's R&D to China which turned out to be a disaster, that is, the bankruptcy of SsangYong in 2009. Geely has learned the lessons from the SsangYong case and chose to leave free rein—at least operationally—to Volvo. Stefan Jacoby, the first CEO, was ejected by Li Shufu in 2012 and replaced by Hakan Samuelsson—who joined the Board in 2011. The year 2013 marked a return to profitability. Li Shufu envisions Volvo as a way of conquering the world. A Volvo model (the S60L) produced in China in Chengdu is now exported to the USA.

In 2015, for the first time in its history, Volvo produced more than half a million cars. It produced 534,000 vehicles in 2016, 570,000 in 2017, 642,000 in 2018, and 705,500 in 2019. Only the Covid stopped this progression with a production down to 662,000 in 2020. The acquisition went obviously well. Also in 2017, building on its success in the recovery of Volvo Cars, Geely took 8% of Volvo Trucks for 3.5 billion €. Geely also took control

(continued)

(continued)
of Lotus and acquired a 49% stake in Malaysian manufacturer Proton.

However, one question remains open: for how long will the former Swedish crown jewel be able to preserve its identity? A common Volvo–Geely platform is under development in Sweden and the design centers are shared. Different expectations will have to be reconciled: Geely wants flashy models for the Chinese market, while Volvo is more discreet. The Chinese and the Swedes have nonetheless found common ground: less polluting engines. In 2017, Volvo announced that it would no longer have 100% gasoline cars in its 2019 catalog, paving the way for 100% electric and hybrid. The year 2017 marked a rebound in profits ($1.67 billion).

In 2018, Li Shufu personally took nearly 10% of Daimler's capital for $9 billion, making him the largest shareholder. He justifies his investment by his desire to cooperate on the electric car and the autonomous car. Daimler was effectively licensed in 2018 to conduct self-driving car tests in China. In the process, Daimler sold 50% of Smart to Geely in 2019—which the Chinese hopes to be able to develop in China. In 2021, total production bypasses the one and a half million vehicles bar; the group aims to produce 3.65 million in 2025. Li Shufu is said to be married to the younger sister of the Chinese first lady (which could explain his astonishing ability to make major deals abroad).

While the takeover of Volvo by Geely made a durable impression, there have not been yet Chinese car players in the automotive industry that have made such significant acquisitions as those made, for example, by Mittal in the steel industry.

The challenges of acquisitions are many. For example, when investing in the USA, a Chinese automotive supplier will have to learn to do business with American unions. More generally, Chinese companies must also learn to be more transparent when they invest in the West. Legal issues (employment contracts, taxation, intellectual property, etc.) can be resolved by calling on local lawyers (specialists in Indian law in India, etc.). The Chinese managers are going to need talent to run the business they buy overseas and face two bottlenecks. The first is in China itself, where a limited number of executives are available for internationalization and ready for expatriation. The second blockage is abroad when recruited executives called to manage these affairs will have to absorb cultural differences; however, the Chinese firms can rely on the diaspora present in the USA, Asia, or Europe. If the pace of learning is high today because Chinese companies are still in a discovery phase, it will undoubtedly be slowed down in the future. And was it already felt (as shown in Fig. 2.3)—due to tensions with the USA and Europe, and campaign of the Chinese authorities against companies with too big debt levels?

China's recent success has been based on what Joseph Schumpeter called "the last mover advantage"; the country knew how to learn and improve what other countries had invented. For a long time, Chinese companies have copied Western products or were inspired by them to offer similar products at half price; recent examples are smartphones from Xiaomi or Haier's HaiPad. This is the sponge metaphor. In fact, once the catching up is done, the copier itself is required to innovate. So Huawei was built on copying Cisco routers and offering inexpensive copies. In the 2000s, Huawei then created its own R&D.

2.3 Building Resources for "Indigenous Innovation"

The Chinese government wants Chinese companies to be able to take their technological autonomy so that exports no longer simply rely on cheap products with low technical content—often designed by foreigners. The country wants to go beyond the stage of simple reproduction. It wants to climb the stairs and establish itself in more sophisticated industries. It is no more and no less than building an economy of technological innovation. Indeed, building indigenous capacity for innovation can be seen as a sine qua non for further Chinese development.

Indigenous Innovation Is Not a New Idea

The Spark program and the 863 program were launched in 1986. The latter's objective was to make China independent from foreign companies in various technological fields; it is still in force and is funded by Beijing. From 1988, the Torch program was launched by the National Commission for Science and Technology which is the structure which preceded the creation of the Ministry of Science and Technology. It aims to accelerate the integration of advanced technologies in industrial manufacturing processes, new materials, biotechnologies, electronics and information technologies, opto-mechanical-electronic integration, new energies, and environmental protection. Several means were implemented: the strengthening of industrial property rights, tax advantages for innovative companies, the creation of partnerships between foreign universities and the Chinese Academy of Sciences (see Chap. 3), Tsinghua University (Chinese MIT), Peking University, and so on.

In 1995, new directions aimed at increasing Chinese R&D capacities to create indigenous technologies and lead to achievements similar to or competing with advanced countries. In 1997, the 973 program covers fundamental research in optics, genomics, nanoscience, brain sciences, paleontology, and chemistry. Much of the basic research would be conducted by the Army—and there, nothing revealed by the Chinese authorities.

In order to develop local innovation, the central government implemented in 2005 the so-called principles of "indigenous innovation." The expression "indigenous innovation" has become the new mantra of Chinese economic development. Innovation, and in particular technological innovation, is traditionally seen by Chinese politicians as an elixir capable of treating all the ills of Chinese society (pollution, demographic unbalance, food insecurity, water stress, etc.) and of ensuring its future development. A lot of support is given to research centers, universities, and also companies to strengthen R&D. This will be depicted in Chap. 3. The idea is to be able to empower companies in different areas. What are the results of this policy?

Mature Industries Are Difficult to Penetrate

While catching up is possible, overtaking foreigners in some technological fields is yet unthinkable. For example, while global automakers have invested in the internal combustion engine for a century, the innovations to come can only be incremental. Therefore, rather than investing in this impossible race, the Chinese companies preferred to bet on a different type of engine. So by investing in R&D on the electric motor and related storage technologies, they are not falling significantly behind and have every chance—the Chinese are looking to skip a generation. Thus, if the game is over in mature industries, Chinese companies retain all their chances of overtaking foreigners in new areas. In this regard, the Internet seems to be a playground where Chinese companies, such as Tencent, are more competitive at least in the local market (see Chap. 5). The technological leap could also potentially be accomplished with the driverless car where China is investing heavily, is served by a sizeable advantage, and relies on a particularly vibrant information technology ecosystem. China can push three or four generations forward. The idea of failing is not a blockage. China leaves with the idea that it is about learning. And that it will catch up on the next generation.

Technological Catch-up Is Effective in Several Sectors

There is an increasing number of innovators in China (Yip & al., 2016; Greeven et al., 2019). Chinese companies are quite convincing in telecommunications (Huawei), high-speed trains (CRRC), or solar panels (Jinko Solar).[2] They are also scoring points in consumer sectors such as home appliances (Haier and Hisense) and the Internet (Baidu, Alibaba, and Tencent).[3] There are technological fields such as 5G where China has clearly taken the lead, whether through telephone equipment manufacturers (Huawei and ZTE) or the base of 800 million smartphone users whose three-fourths have converted to mobile payment. Lithium batteries are another example of Chinese leadership. The lithium-ion

---

[2] The case of solar panels and the high-speed train are exposed in Chap. 6.
[3] The Internet case is presented in Chap. 5.

segment has been dominated until recently by the Japanese and South Koreans, who became world number two and three in 2020. The Chinese success is explained by the size of its local battery market and the control over raw material. The Chinese government wants to impose on manufacturers a minimum percentage to do with zero-emission vehicles; Americans and Europeans are not, however, sitting idly by. China also has its chances in renewable energies, fin-tech, autonomous vehicles, artificial intelligence, and—in an emerging field—the Internet of Things (i.e., the connection of machines to each other). Automobile manufacturers such as ChangAn and BAIC, but also the Internet platforms, such as Alibaba and Baidu, are in the run.

The Challenge Remains in Several Sectors

Chinese companies are lagging behind in automotive design, pharmaceuticals, biotechnologies, specialty chemicals, or the semiconductor industry—all of which have been identified as priorities by the government. These are sectors that require innovation from science (this lack of investment is perhaps the expression of a Chinese preference for the short term). And, China is lagging behind in fundamental research and disruptive innovation.

The "just good-enough" policy which often prevails in China is not sufficient in these industries. For example, although the number of Chinese publications in the life sciences has exploded since the early 2000s and if several Chinese companies are in the ranks (such as Hutchison, Chi-Med, or Simcere), China has not yet brought an innovative and recognized drug to the global market. Innovative drugs come primarily from the USA and, to a lesser extent, from Europe. Moreover, the number of new innovative drugs remains very limited. For example, the US FDA only approves 20–25 per year. In biotech, the USA is the undisputed leader. For many Chinese biotechnology startups, the challenge is to move from the stage of fast follower to that of true innovator. Thus, in biotechnology, if Chinese companies are still catching up, a few isolated cases such as Nanjing Legend Biotech or Innovative Cellular Therapeutics are at the origin of progress in cell therapy for the treatment of cancer. China, on the other hand, is the world's largest producer and exporter of active pharmaceutical ingredients.

Chinese firms are also lagging behind in the design of aircraft engines. All means are good to fill the gap; thus, in 2017, the Chinese Skyrizon became the main shareholder of the Ukrainian engine manufacturer Motor Sich—a company of 20,000 people, which notably supplies Antonov. But, at the beginning of 2021, Ukrainian authorities refused to approve the deal. That's a clear illustration that acquisition strategies are not the panacea to appropriate technologies.

China is so famous for exporting that we forget that it imports too. An overwhelming share of semiconductors consumed in China are purchased in the USA, South Korea, and Malaysia, among others. While China accounts for 55% of world demand, 85% of its needs are met by imports—which exceeded $300 billion in 2020 (more than oil imports). For decades, China has sought to shake off its reliance on the West for semiconductors. Neither acceptable methods (joint-ventures, business takeovers, etc.) nor less honorable ones (espionage, intellectual property theft, etc.) have been sufficient so far. The USA still has the lead but China has narrowed the gap in semiconductor production and design. This dependence was exemplified by the case of ZTE, which the USA threatened in 2018 of no longer supplying components and which consequently raised questions about its survival. ZTE could have sunk, but chose to pay a fine to suspend the sanctions.

It is because of this weakness that the Chinese government has ambitious investment plans to increase local production of semiconductors. The key player is Semiconductor Manufacturing International Corporation (SMIC), which ranked among the top five foundries. Another Chinese player is Tsinghua Unigroup—majority-owned by Tsinghua Holdings (100% owned by Tsinghua University) and 49% by a private group (Beijing Jiankun Investment). Tsinghua Unigroup has committed tens of billions of dollars for the buyout of foreign manufacturers (including Integrated Silicon Solutions); however, it failed to take over US giant Micron Technology.

Toward a Breakthrough?

The emphasis on R&D places a heavy responsibility on Chinese companies: ensuring the country's move upmarket and solving its societal problems such as damage to the natural environment. The innovations that emerge from the Chinese fabric remain for the moment mainly innovations of the incremental type, resulting from development or applied research activities. Just because Huawei brought what was once the world's thinnest cell phone to market doesn't mean the company invented a new model. It will undoubtedly take a little while before a Chinese company arrives with a genuine breakthrough innovation, and even more with a disruptive innovation, that is, an innovation with high transformational value such as digital images or even the iPhone, iPod, or iPad.

China can get ahead in specific areas, however. In the field of traditional Chinese medicine, Tu Youyou was the first Chinese scientist to earn the Nobel Prize in medicine in 2015 for her work on artemisinin for the treatment of malaria. Quantum communication, with applications ranging from defense to finance, is another example. China has already surpassed the USA regarding the number of patents and its research budget in quantum communication. The launch in 2016 of the Micius satellite (named after a former Chinese philosopher and scientist) testified to its experiments in quantum physics, which could pave the way for communications impossible to hack by transmitting indecipherable codes from space to earth. Any attack on a quantum channel alters the information transmitted and consequently informs the parties. Secure quantum communications should thus be possible on ground between Beijing and Shanghai in the future. The Jinan Institute of Quantum Technology is working on it. And in the field of quantum computing, the University of Science and Technology of China reached quantum supremacy when competing with Google. If China were to continue down this path, it could hold a major advantage in the future.

2.4 China Succeeded in Achieving Astonishing Results in Publications and Patents

China has outpaced the USA on many criteria. This includes the number of scientific articles produced and the number of patents.

A Booming Publications Record

Progress is visible in the number of scientific articles published by Chinese professors and researchers. According to the US National Science Foundation, the production of science and engineering articles in the world has significantly increased, moving from 1072 million in 2000 to 2556 in 2018 (+5% per year). The main explanation lies into the booming of articles from China (13% per year from 1996 to 2018) as illustrated by data in Table 2.3.

Things have changed very quickly. Chinese academic entities produced a meager 33,000 articles yearly in 1996. It took only 20 years for China

Table 2.3 Science and engineering articles in all fields (1996–2018)

Publication year	USA	European Union	China	India	Japan	Rest of world	Σ
1996	304,804	328,646	33,237	19,094	88,398	198,567	972,746
1997	305,060	346,119	37,084	19,557	91,843	208,817	1,008,480
1998	298,570	349,922	43,317	19,984	92,464	213,714	1,017,971
1999	294,477	348,540	45,129	21,190	94,422	220,084	1,023,842
2000	304,782	366,366	53,064	21,771	97,048	228,922	1,071,953
2001	305,613	372,466	70,439	22,948	96,498	240,070	1,108,034
2002	319,308	383,951	74,016	24,853	98,555	255,000	1,155,683
2003	329,399	395,804	86,912	27,296	100,691	276,697	1,216,799
2004	353,853	420,297	120,363	29,348	103,446	301,441	1,328,748
2005	384,573	461,700	165,336	33,516	111,708	336,989	1,493,822
2006	385,515	482,096	189,949	38,515	112,127	366,123	1,574,325
2007	391,910	508,022	215,207	43,627	109,982	398,404	1,667,152
2008	393,979	528,938	249,049	48,998	108,241	426,645	1,755,850
2009	399,350	551,184	286,372	54,798	109,131	456,280	1,857,115
2010	408,817	563,296	312,517	62,437	109,025	492,713	1,948,805
2011	423,959	585,516	326,771	74,143	111,258	530,193	2,051,840
2012	427,997	609,160	329,015	80,493	109,644	553,695	2,110,004
2013	429,570	620,915	359,274	86,348	108,996	573,953	2,179,056
2014	433,192	635,766	390,396	96,426	105,856	602,490	2,264,126
2015	429,989	633,309	407,975	101,813	101,307	619,700	2,294,093
2016	427,265	635,292	438,349	112,167	101,297	662,810	2,377,180
2017	432,216	635,882	473,439	121,631	101,084	701,437	2,465,689
2018	422,808	622,125	528,263	135,788	98,793	748,183	2,555,960

Source: Publications Output: U.S. Trends and International Comparisons, Science & Engineering Indicators, The US National Science Foundation (https://nsf.gov/statistics/seind/)

to surpass the USA in terms of the number of scientific publications: 438,000 versus 427,000 in 2016. However, US scientific works remain the most cited. This is explained by the language and also because the best journals are often based in the USA.

Registered Patents Challenge US Supremacy

China did not exist on the global R&D map a few years ago: it filed less than 50,000 patents per year until 1999 and less than 100,000 patents per year until 2003. It was the peak of counterfeiting. For over 30 years, the USA and Japan held the top two places on the podium for patent applicants—with Europe struggling to reach third place. The USA registered between 300,000 and 430,000 patents per year from 1990 to 2006. And, Japan went to more than 400,000 per year.

Under the impetus of the "indigenous innovation" program, the Chinese political power wanted Chinese companies to engage in R&D and the filing of patents; the barrier of disdain for the prevailing patent had to be overcome. The government encouraged them to learn about patent filing procedures with "utility patents" (these are equivalent to what the Germans call "Gebrauchsmuster," but which do not exist in the USA). Utility patents relate to improvements in existing products or technologies and are therefore low substance patents. This boost from the government produced major results as shown in Table 2.4. Records have skyrocketed. In 2011, according to the World Intellectual Property Office (WIPO), China surpassed the USA for patent applications: 526,000 were filed in China versus 504,000 were filed in the USA, and 343,000 in Japan.

Companies like Huawei Technologies, ZTE, or Tencent are now well established in the global rankings of patent applicants. We can certainly criticize the value of the patents filed, but a major movement has indeed been initiated. And the trend continues. The 1.5 million mark was exceeded in 2018 (versus 597,000 in the USA). China is challenging the American technological superpower in this regard. However, few Chinese patents are filed outside of China; the number of triadic patents (filed in the USA, Japan, and Europe) is absolutely ridiculous. Here too, things are changing; and Chinese firms are filing more and more internationally, as shown by statistics from the European Patent Office (EPO).

2 The China Public Policy for Technology Creation

Table 2.4 Total patent applications (direct and PCT national phase entries)

(Thousands)	Brazil	China	Europe	India	Japan	Korea	Russia	USA
1997	16	25	264	10	392	93	23	220
1998	16	47	278	9	402	75	25	237
1999	17	59	296	5	406	81	28	266
2000	17	52	321	9	437	102	32	296
2001	18	63	330	11	439	105	34	326
2002	17	80	317	11	421	106	33	334
2003	16	105	324	13	413	119	35	342
2004	17	130	323	17	423	140	30	357
2005	18	173	326	24	427	161	32	391
2006	20	211	333	29	409	166	38	426
2007	22	245	339	35	396	172	39	456
2008	23	290	346	37	391	171	42	456
2009	22	391	323	40	349	170	42	456
2010	25	315	343	34	345	164	39	490
2011	29	526	334	42	343	179	41	504
2012	30	652	346	43	343	189	44	543
2013	31	825	346	43	328	205	45	572
2014	30	928	346	43	326	210	40	579
2015	30	1102	360	46	319	214	46	589
2016	28	1339	355	45	318	209	42	606
2017	26	1382	356	47	318	205	37	607
2018	25	1542	362	50	314	210	38	597
2019	25	1401	364	54	308	219	36	621
2020	24	1497	358	57	288	227	35	597

PCT: Patent Cooperation Treaty
Source: World Intellectual Property Organization

2.5 Conclusion

This chapter has shown that the Chinese government had consistently pushed for technology over the last 40 years. After a first phase of importing technologies from advanced countries, Chinese firms have started to absorb the imported knowledge. This was followed by replication. The moto is now clearly to innovate locally. As a matter of fact, statistics show the tremendous progress accomplished backward, that is, at the beginning of the creative process with a surge in scientific publications. The same astonishing explosion occurred forward with the number of patents.

We can certainly note that the citation rate of scientific publications of the Chinese remains low. We can certainly criticize the youth of science and technology parks. We can certainly criticize the level of patents filed. But, the movement has indeed been set in motion. But, we have to acknowledge that China is no longer in the shadow of the great scientific nations even if Chinese scientific output has still low impact.

What happened? How can we explain such a major change? My hypothesis is that this situation is the output of the efforts made to bundle all the necessary ingredients to make a successful national system of innovation. This is what I intend to demonstrate in Chap. 3.

References

Greeven, M., George, S. Y., & Wei, W. (2019). *Pioneers, hidden champions, change makers and underdogs: Lessons from China's innovators*. The MIT Press.
Jolly, D. (2004). Bartering technology for local resources in exogamic Sino-foreign joint ventures. *R & D Management, 34*(4), 389–407.
Jolly, D. (2005). The exogamic nature of Sino-foreign joint ventures. *Asia Pacific Journal of Management, 22*(3), 285–306.
Jolly, D. (2006). Sino-foreign joint ventures: From exogamy to endogamy. *Journal of Technology Management in China, 1*(2), 131–146.
Jolly, D., & Thérin, F. (2007). "New venture technology sourcing: Exploring the effect of absorptive capacity, learning attitude and past performance", innovation: Management. *Policy & Practice, 9*(3–4), 235–248.
Kim, L. (1997). *Imitation to innovation: The dynamics of Korea's technological learning* (p. 301). Harvard Business School Press.
Luo, Y., & Tung, R. L. (2007). International expansion of emerging market enterprises: A springboard perspective. *Journal of International Business Studies, 38*(4), 481–498.
Mazloomi Khamseh, H., & Jolly, D. (2008). Knowledge transfer in alliances: Determinant factors. *The Journal of Knowledge Management, 12*(1), 37–50.
WIPO (World Intellectual Property Organization). *Statistical country profiles*. https://www.wipo.int/ipstats/en/statistics/country_profile/.
Yip, G. S., & Bruce, M. K. (2016). *China's next strategic advantage: From imitation to innovation*. The MIT Press.

3

The Chinese National System of Innovation

Abstract This chapter suggests that China's achievements in terms of technology creation result from the bundling of seven key assets. ① A group of leading research universities combined with ② public research centers now produce the largest number of scientific articles in the world. ③ Infrastructures such as science and technology parks, clusters and incubators, were created to foster the development of ④ an impressive number of high-tech startups and a record number of unicorns. ⑤ A dynamic sector for the financing of technological innovation has emerged in parallel to subsidies distributed by different levels of government. ⑥ Both Chinese public and private companies, as well as foreign companies, cumulatively achieved the second largest R&D budget in the world. ⑦ Innovators are now protected by a regulatory framework comparable to what can be found outside China.

Keywords R&D • Technology creation • Technological innovation • Stakeholders of innovation • National system of innovation

This chapter relies on the concept of "national system of innovation" developed by Nelson (1993) and Nelson & Rosenberg (1993). It depicts the major stakeholders of the Chinese national system of innovation, their profiles, latest moves, and ambitions. It shows that China was able to bundle all the necessary seven ingredients for technology creation listed below:

1. An efficient education system with some leading research universities. Deeply embedded Confucianism roots give true respect for education and learning.
2. A powerful China Academy of Sciences driving a strong network of public research centers.
3. A set of infrastructures, including science and technology parks (inspired by the US model) with the expected clusters and incubators. Shenzhen is the most impressive example.
4. An outstanding number of high-tech startups, and unicorns.
5. Multiple sources for financing technology creation.
6. An increasing number of companies (Chinese public, and private, and foreign) investing in R&D.
7. A regulatory framework, inspired from existing Western frameworks, to protect innovators.

The chapter introduces several case studies and relies on several sources, including research conducted by the author on Chinese science parks (Jolly & Zhu, 2012), on technology creation by Chinese firms (Shan & Jolly, 2011, 2013) and by foreign multinational companies in China (Jolly et al., 2015, 2016; Jolly & Masetti, 2016).

3.1 An Efficient Education System

A Gigantic Brainpower Machine

Primary and secondary education in China is first and foremost a big deal: 200 million children and 15 million teachers. In addition, education is key in the Confucianist culture. There is a cult of school performance across the country, exemplified by the extraordinary cases of Shanghai, Beijing, and the provinces of Jiangsu and Zhejiang, recognized by the Pisa ranking (Program for International Students Assessment) of the OECD (i.e., the 34 richest countries on the planet of which China is not a member, but observer). As shown in Table 3.1, China consistently rates higher than the OECD average for the three criteria of literacy (reading, mathematics, science) over the period displayed. Japan is the only one which competes with China, and the USA is behind. With such a massive reservoir of brainpower, it would not be surprising to find some candidates for future Nobel prizes. Yet, Chinese data is limited to only the wealthiest areas; if data from all provinces (i.e., including the poor and rural ones) is taken into account, the result will plummet.

China claims an average literacy rate of 75%; the rate even climbs to 99% in the 15–24 age group. The logic is utilitarian—no room for dreamers. Chinese education is known to prioritize knowledge learned by heart. The method of memorization is the absolute standard in elementary and secondary schools. Students must learn to write. There is no other way than repeating tirelessly, and in addition memorizing tirades from ancient texts.

Table 3.1 China in the PISA rankings (2012–2018)[a]

		2012	2015	2018
Reading literacy	China (*)	570	494	555
	OECD	496	493	487
	USA	498	497	505
	Japan	538	516	504
	Russia	475	495	479
Mathematical literacy	China (*)	613	531	591
	OECD	494	490	489
	USA	481	470	478
	Japan	536	532	527
	Russia	482	487	488
Scientific literacy	China (*)	580	518	590
	OECD	501	493	489
	USA	497	496	502
	Japan	547	538	529
	Russia	486	487	478

(*): 2012: data for Shanghai, 2015–2018: data for Beijing, Shanghai, Jiangsu, and Zhejiang
Source: OECD, https://www.oecd.org/pisa/data/
[a]OECD country members decided to postpone the PISA 2021 assessment to 2022

The "Gaokao" Filter: The Chinese High-School Diploma

Education in China is also known for the importance given to the "Gaokao," the Chinese high-school diploma, which is an essential step in the academic career of young Chinese (prior to the diploma, they must pass the "Zhongkao," which is the equivalent of the primary school certificate). As shown in Table 3.2, each year, approximately ten million of candidates across the country undergo enormous pressure in taking the three-day examination required to achieve the diploma. The number of candidates was on the decline (9.4 million in 2017 against 10.5 million in 2008); but, seems to have recently recovered.

Access to universities is determined by the ranking; universities like Tsinghua (a kind of Chinese MIT) or Beida attract the best students (it is said that it is more difficult to enter Tsinghua than to enter Harvard or Yale). These same universities are moving up the world rankings in education, research, and international connections—and not just in the Shanghai University rankings; they develop formidable firepower. Some universities in foreign countries such as Australia, Italy, and the USA also use "Gaokao" results as criteria for admission.

The interest of students in money is revealed by their choices of major. In 15 years (1998–2012), the proportion of young Chinese embarking on the path of economics and management has increased considerably (reaching one-fourth of students in 2012)—not to mention the growth in the number of MBA students. During this period, fundamental sciences attracted students in proportion (less than 10% of the registered ones). The same can be said for medical studies where these professionals do not have the same social status or prestige, or the same income, as in the West.

Universities in China: Volume, But Not Only

China operates a very large number of universities—about 3000 all around the country: 2956 higher educational institutes according to the

Table 3.2 Number of students registered for the Gaokao (in million)

2016	2017	2018	2019	2020	2021
9.40	9.40	9.75	10.31	10.71	10.78

Source: Chinese Ministry of Education

Ministry of Education, split into 2688 regular universities, and 268 for adults. In 2011, they were "only" 2200 universities. The increase in the number of institutes is directly proportional to the number of students.

Tables 3.3 and 3.4 show trends from 2013 to 2019. These are quite positive. The number of students registered is increasing—with the exception of adult education (also growing over the period but with a more complex trend). It gained almost 10 million over seven years, from 38.88 million to 48.45 million.

The same model is reproduced by the number of students graduating each year.

As illustrated by Fig. 3.1, most Chinese universities are teaching universities. A relatively small number are research universities. In 2019, the number of full-time faculty in (2688) regular universities reached 1.7 million. This gives a good ratio of the number of students per professor. Yet, another feature is that only 75% of professors have a master's degree or above. As such, this statistic shows the limited interest for research.

Table 3.3 Higher education in China: number of students enrolled

(in million)	2013	2014	2015	2016	2017	2018	2019
Postgraduates	1.79	1.85	1.91	1.98	2.64	2.73	2.86
Undergraduates in regular universities	24.68	25.48	26.25	26.96	27.54	28.31	30.32
Undergraduates in adult universities	6.26	6.53	6.36	5.84	5.44	5.91	6.69
Web-based undergraduates	6.15	6.31	6.28	6.45	7.36	8.26	8.58
Total	38.88	40.17	40.80	41.23	42.98	45.21	48.45

Source: Ministry of Education—The People's Republic of China
http://en.moe.gov.cn/documents/statistics/2019/national/

Table 3.4 Higher education in China: number of students graduating per year

(in million)	2013	2014	2015	2016	2017	2018	2019
Postgraduates	0.51	0.54	0.55	0.56	0.58	0.60	0.61
Undergraduates in regular universities	6.39	6.59	6.81	7.04	7.36	7.53	7.59
Undergraduates in adult universities	2.00	2.21	2.36	2.44	2.47	2.18	2.13
Web-based undergraduates	1.56	1.66	1.80	1.87	1.78	1.95	2.32
Total	10.46	11.00	11.52	11.91	12.19	12.26	12.65

Source: Ministry of Education—The People's Republic of China
http://en.moe.gov.cn/documents/statistics/2019/national/

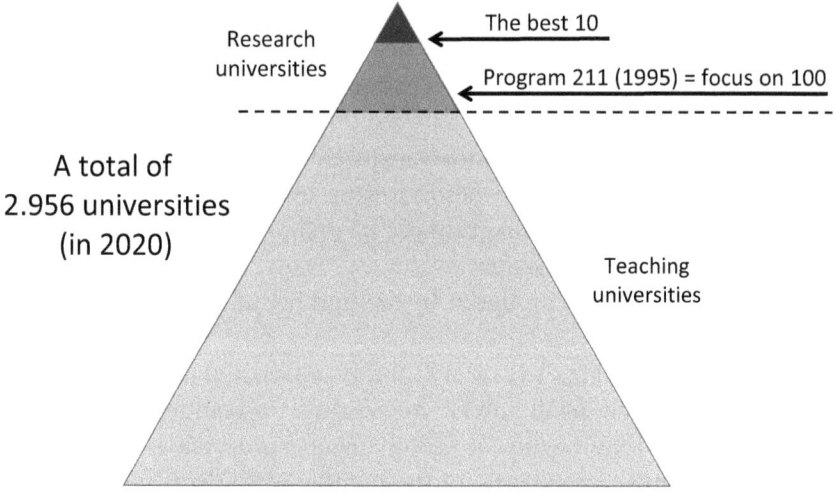

Fig. 3.1 Investments in universities

Over the last 30 years, several governmental programs have aimed at stimulating Chinese universities—especially those which are research universities. In 1995, the Ministry of Education launched the 211 program, which targeted a group of 100 universities to help them to push their research standards. The aim of project 985—launched in May 1998 and operational until 2011—was to help selected Chinese universities to reach the status of world-class universities. It helped to focus on key disciplines, to recruit top professors and to reinforce research. More recently, the Double First Class, a program launched by the government in 2015, is to foster the development of a selected group of 42 universities. Funding comes from central and also local governments. All those programs helped to significantly raise the standard of the top Chinese universities; one limit is they tend to widen the gap between participating universities and others.

The top 20 Chinese universities are listed in Table 3.5 according to the well-known Shanghai Ranking. The individual score aggregates research output, research influence, international collaborations, research quality, and international academic awards. This ranking of the top universities has been relatively stable over the years (and is not very different from other rankings, like QS, for example).

Table 3.5 Top 20 Chinese universities

Rank	University	Location	Score
1	Tsinghua University	Beijing	969
2	Peking University	Beijing	855
3	Zhejiang University	Zhejiang	769
4	Shanghai Jiao Tong University	Shanghai	723
5	Nanjing University	Jiangsu	655
6	Fudan University	Shanghai	650
7	University of Science & Technology of China	Anhui	577
8	Huazhong University of Science & Technology	Hubei	574
9	Wuhan University	Hubei	568
10	Xi'an Jiaotong University	Shaanxi	538
11	Harbin Institute of Technology	Heilongjiang	523
12	Sun Yat-Sen University	Guangdong	519
13	Beijing Normal University	Beijing	518
14	Sichuan University	Sichuan	516
15	Beihang University	Beijing	514
16	Tongji University	Shanghai	508
17	Southeast University	Jiangsu	488
18	Renmin University of China	Beijing	488
19	Beijing Institute of Technology	Beijing	474
20	Nankai University	Tianjin	465

Source: Shanghai Ranking, https://www.shanghairanking.com/
Note: of the first 20, only 4 (Huazhong, Wuhan, Xi'an, Sichuan) are not located on the coast

The Weaknesses of the Education System

Not surprisingly, the rural education system has fewer resources than urban education. It is also in the countryside that child labor is said to be most frequent. Quotas by region favor students who want to enter a university in their city. But, as the best universities are mostly on the coast, students from other provinces have to fit into the limited quota offered to them.

Another weakness of the Chinese education system is that the qualifications of graduates do not always match the needs of the market. The university is not open to internships; consequently, the period of adaptation of young graduates to professional practice is quite long. In addition, it does not prepare young people to work in groups.

Thus, more and more Chinese parents, at least among those who can afford it, are sending their children to study abroad—which may show a willingness to understand other complementary systems, but also reveal a lack of confidence in their own system. The point is particularly visible in the USA. The number of Chinese students was only 68,000 in 2006–2007; the figure rose to 275,000 Chinese in 2014 (out of a total of 886,000 foreign students). With 370,000 Chinese students, they comprised the first contingent in 2019–2020 in the USA, which welcomed a million foreign students (India is in the second place with 202,000 students). US universities welcome these new clients and can charge them tuition fees two to three times higher than those charged to American students. Professors are sometimes less enthusiastic when communication problems emerge and especially when the contingents of Chinese students in the same class are close to or even exceed half the number of students. After completing their studies, some wish to stay in their host country. Yet there are many more opportunities for young Chinese in China than in the USA struggling to regenerate.

Change of Context

The situation is, however, tense in China for young graduates—especially since the number of graduates has increased significantly (cf. Table 3.4). The slowdown in economic growth is not helping the situation. A university degree is no longer a guarantee of employment. Moreover, as already mentioned, these young people do not necessarily have the skills expected by employers. Their training means that they are not inclined to question established doctrines and bring out original ideas. The unemployment rate for young graduates (over 7%) is above average (officially 4% in the city). The Chinese communist party fears the emergence of a generation of frustrated ambitious people. In fact, it is with young people that the gap with Xi Jinping and his peers is most marked; they do not appreciate the interference of politicians on their lives.

However, even when their career has started, individuals are not afraid to invest in training since the growth in their salary allows them to very quickly recover what is not an expense but an investment. In this context, where things are becoming more complicated (slowdown in growth, rising costs, tensions with the USA, technological wave, Western penetration, etc.), the authorities see traditional Chinese values as a base on which to anchor. This is the "guoxue" movement (literally, home education). More weight is given to the teaching of the texts of Confucius, to the poetry of the Tang dynasty, to painting, to calligraphy, and so forth.

3.2   A Powerful Chinese Academy of Sciences

A Recent Comeback to Science

Founded in 1949, the Chinese Academy of Sciences (CAS) is the country's highest scientific body. It was built on the remains of the Sinica Academy created in 1928 by Tchang Kai-shek to coordinate scientific research (the Sinica Academy was transferred to Taipei in October 1949). CAS was also inspired by the Soviet Academy of Sciences. It must have suffered during the dark period of the Cultural Revolution (1966–1976) when it was better to be "red" than a scientific expert. Fundamental research had been neglected in Mao's time because it was considered too theoretical and without immediate practical application for the masses; research was applied in nature (without a race for a Nobel Prize). China would have to wait until 1978 and Deng Xiaoping for new policies in favor of science and technology.

Steering Both Political and Technical Issues

CAS is now one of the two big players in science and technology, with the Ministry of Science and Technology and the research institutes managed by ministries. CAS reports directly to the Council of State Affairs. It benefits from the advice of a group of 700 academics. It has six sections: (a) mathematical and physical sciences, (b) life sciences and medicine, (c) chemistry, (d) earth sciences, (e) technological sciences, (f) information sciences. It represents more than 100 research centers. The Shanghai Institute for Biological Sciences (SIBS) and the more recently created Shanghai Advanced Research Institute (SARI) are examples of those public research laboratories within the scope of CAS. There is even a unit opened by the Institut Pasteur within CAS. In addition, CAS has two universities of its own.

In total, in 2020, CAS employs 67,900 people, including 56,000 scientists and engineers. Budget has been considerably expanded. In 2009, it reached $3 billion; it was already seven times the level of 1998. In 2020, the budget exceeded $15 billion. The state funds 50% to cover costs and salaries. The other 50% comes from tenders.

Fundamental Research Stays Behind at CAS

The CAS, like the Chinese universities engaged in research, is still today more oriented toward applied research than toward fundamental research. This Chinese weakness has its advantages: Chinese researchers are pragmatic and connected with practice, which makes contact with manufacturers easier. Thus, one can find pilot industrial production units in CAS institutes developed for testing (which these institutes incidentally use as sources of income). There are also almost always professors who have started their own businesses while maintaining their position at the university, which for them is a genuine source of additional income that will far exceed their basic income.

Lenovo (ex-Legend IT) is an entity that was spun off from CAS. Another well-known case of a spin-off is the Beijing Genomics Institute. Founded by CAS, the company has been based in Shenzhen since 2007. It was the first to decode the genome of the rice. It performs large-scale genetic sequencing for the study of the human genome—data that could prove useful in discovering new drugs.

The Chinese Academy of Engineering

Besides CAS, the Chinese Academy of Engineering (CAE) was established in 1994 with around 100 members. It reports directly to the Council of State Affairs. Its headquarters are in Beijing. It is made up of personalities elected by members of the academy's divisions. Applicants are scientists who have had significant achievements in engineering or technology. The CAE welcomes several foreign members, also elected. Membership grew to nearly 800 members in 2012.

CAE is a kind of think-tank that the government consults to feed its thinking. It is not a research institution. Its purpose is to conduct studies and advise policymakers on major public policy issues affecting engineering and technology. In particular, it has conducted studies on sustainable energy development, sustainable development of water resources, and also regional studies. It is also in charge of the implementation of programs imposed by the government in this field and of international cooperation. CAE is organized into eight divisions: (a) automotive mechanics and engineering, (b) information and electronics, (c) chemistry, metallurgy, and materials, (d) civil engineering, hydraulics, and architecture, (e) agriculture, (f) environment, light industry, and textiles, (g) medicine and health, and (h) engineering management.

3.3 Science and Technology Parks

More Than 100 Parks Were Created

The central and provincial governments have invested considerable sums so that Chinese private and public companies, like foreign firms, can engage in research and development. As already mentioned, this is nothing less than fostering indigenous technological creation to break technological dependence on the outside. In order to accomplish this, geographical locations dedicated to technology creation are needed. China has accelerated the opening of science and technology parks for more than 20 years. The 100 science and technology parks (most of them recently created) are unsurprisingly highly concentrated around the first-tier cities: the regions of Beijing, Shanghai and the Yangzi delta, and Guangzhou and Shenzhen (Jolly & Zhu, 2012). This number has grown to 169 in 2020. Zhangjiang Hi-tech Park in Shanghai and Zhongguancun Science Park in Beijing are the best-known science and technology parks. Each has its own clusters, that is, agglomerations of related competitors, suppliers, customers, public research institutes, and universities. The first is a focal point for chemistry, pharmacy, and semiconductor. The second is known for information technology, space, and biotechnology. Baidu, the Chinese Internet search engine that overwhelmingly dominates the

Chinese market, is headquartered in Zhongguancun in Beijing. Zhongguancun incorporates about ten different science parks—such as Haidian, the first park to be labeled in 1988 under the Torch program, and also the birthplace of Lenovo. The Shenzhen park (Guangdong) and Suzhou Industrial Park (Jiangsu) are also well known, but more for their industrial side; however, they are increasingly engaging in R&D.

Incubators are another key physical asset. While there were only around 100 incubators in 2000, the number reached 1500 in 2013 (according to the Torch program). The figure topped 8000 in 2017. Once shy when it came to technology, China is now firmly established on the global map of technology creation.

All of these parks have attracted large Chinese and foreign companies. For example, most of the world's major pharmaceutical companies have opened an R&D center in the "Pharma Valley" within Zhangjiang Hi-tech Park in Shanghai. The large science and technology parks are home to first-class universities (e.g., Tsinghua University and Peking University are both located within the Zhongguancun perimeter) and also important public research centers. Some are good ecosystems for startups. The next step could be the establishment of science and technology parks abroad to accommodate Chinese companies.

A Techno-Driven City: The Example of Shenzhen

Deng Xiaoping wanted the city of Shenzhen on the Pearl River Delta (Guangdong) to compete with the border city of Hong Kong. This is one of the very first four special economic zones (SEZs) created in China to attract foreign companies. The territory stretches over 80 kilometers from east to west and about 40 kilometers from north to south. The city had only 20,000 inhabitants in 1979. The population had increased to 300,000 inhabitants in 1980. This figure reached more than 3 million in 1993 and 6 million in 2004. In 2009, the megalopolis had more than 10 million inhabitants. The population reached 15 million in 2017. It is probably the fastest growing city in the world. It is therefore a city of migrants. Shenzhen with its satellites (Dongguan, Huizhou, and Zhongshan), Canton, and Hong Kong form the "Greater Bay Area" which could one day rival the San Francisco Bay Area. The 40th anniversary of the Shenzhen Special Economic Zone (SEZ) in 2020 justified Xi Jinping's visit.

Shenzhen is one of the pioneering models of Chinese science and technology parks. Its main industries are electronics, pharmaceuticals, biotechnology, textiles, and jewelry. Firms like Huawei, ZTE, Tencent, BYD, and also BGI (formerly known as Beijing Genomics Institute) are headquartered in Shenzhen. Huawei occupies a central place in this ecosystem. There are over 2000 manufacturers of electronic products and components. Shenzhen is also the headquarters of Da Jiang Innovations (DJI), the world's largest drone maker that sells both drones to individuals and to businesses (e.g., it sells drones to Chinese farmers to spread pesticides). It also sells drones in the USA to both individuals and government agencies. Shenzhen welcomes foreign companies such as Sanofi, Véolia, Schneider, and especially the Taiwanese Foxconn.

Shenzhen has brought together all the necessary ingredients for economic development: infrastructure, finance, insurance, real estate, and so on. Shenzhen is home to China's second deep-water container terminal. Taking advantage of tax-free zones and port infrastructures, several companies have made logistics a lucrative business and developed expertise in the management of different modes of transport. A considerable number of metro lines have been built; it exceeds 400 kilometers since 2020. Shenzhen is only 15 minutes from Hong Kong. The city has its own airline, Shenzhen Airlines, a private company of 14,000 people (with around 100 planes, it is the fifth largest in China); however, it had difficulty after the arrest of several of its executives for corruption and was finally acquired by Air China. A new, state-of-the-art airport was commissioned in 2013 at the western end of the city, replacing the old 1991 airport—deemed already aging. Shenzhen is home to the second mainland China stock exchange (opened in 1991); it receives more private companies, younger and smaller than the Shanghai Stock Exchange. Shenzhen has its bank, the Shenzhen Development Bank. The Ping An insurance company is building a 599-meter skyscraper there. In 2013, in response to central government directives, the Guangdong authorities set up China's first carbon emission credits market in Shenzhen (inspired by European and North American experiences).

The GDP per capita (2020) reaches $22,800. Shenzhen's economy overtook Hong Kong's in 2018. The city has the highest minimum wage in China. With the rising cost of labor, companies are responding by relocating (to neighboring Vietnam, for example) or by investing in robotization. Despite the slowdown in the Chinese economy, housing prices continue to rise. Shenzhen achieves a growth rate significantly higher than the national average (two points higher in 2015). The city is climbing the technological ladder. There will be 450 incubators which will house 8500 startups. The new investments are being made in drones, 3D printers, and robotization. Shenzhen is now home to a design museum that China Merchants Group wanted and that was designed by a Japanese architect. In the heart of Shenzhen is Baishizhou, an enclave inherited from a collective farm from the Mao era. It is home to 150,000 Chinese citizens who benefit from low rents. These urban villages have so far resisted invaders, who would turn them into a new area of modern housing and commerce. However, sooner or later, they are undoubtedly bound for demolition (inspired by European and North American experiences).

3.4 A Myriad of Hi-tech Startups and Unicorns

Profusion

China has recently taken the first place in several rankings: particularly in terms of the number of scientific publications, the number of patents filed (as shown in Chap. 2), and the number of startups (Petti & Ederer, 2012). These startups can be found in science and technology parks such as Zhongguancun, Zhangjiang, Shenzhen, and Suzhou. Ximalaya is an interesting example. This startup was created in 2012. Its activity is an Internet application accessible from a smartphone that allows podcast sharing. It claims 80 million active users per month. With 700 employees, it was valued at $3.5 billion in 2021. It competes with other startups like Qingting and Lizhi. Unsurprisingly, startups are the targets of large groups seeking to access innovation. The acquisition of startups is widely practiced by groups like Alibaba and Tencent. E-commerce has become common for investing in a large number of startups.

Many Chinese startups have become unicorns, that is, startups valued over $1 billion. In 2018, there are 168 unicorns in China valued at $628 billion. They are found in many emerging sectors in China: new energies, Fintech, social media, artificial intelligence, clean-tech, logistics, tourism, block-chain, and cloud. ByteDance is an example (see Chap. 5).

Internet, Pharma, Biotech, Artificial Intelligence, Electric Cars

A number of startups have emerged in a number of activities with high technological content such as the Internet, pharmacy, new energies, electric cars, autonomous vehicles, technologies applied to finance and artificial intelligence. Chinese startups have also emerged in the automotive sector and are trying to emulate the success of Tesla and BYD, such as Faraday Future, Nio, Bytou, Xpeng Motors, and WM Motorset. Like many companies in emerging sectors, electric car startups often flirt with bankruptcy as soon as the funds required for development are no longer there. Several startups have also emerged in the autonomous car, for example, Pony.ai, NavInfo, Neolix, or TuSimple. In Chinese pharmacy, startups like Shanghai Blood Products, Zensun, BeiGene, Chi-Med, and Wuxi Biologics would like to be recognized. Shanghai Blood Products was thus voted one of the most innovative firms in the world by Forbes (2017). The diaspora (see Chap. 2) plays a key role with startups. In fields such as pharmaceuticals and biotechnologies, it is the *haigui* (Chinese people who went abroad for a few years) who have created most of the startups in the field in China. For many Chinese startups from biotechnology, the challenge is to move from the "fast-follower" stage to that of a true innovator.

Success and Failures

Chinese startups are raising more funds today than American ones. Investment funds such as Sequoia Capital, Sinovation, Panda Capital, Tiger Global, Silver Lake, … buy or take stakes in Chinese startups. The Zhongguancun Science and Technology Park in Beijing is a particularly fertile ground in this area; the park concentrates many universities and research centers whose professors and researchers are typically creators of startups. They provide a work environment that is second to none in Silicon Valley. But, startup entrepreneurs may sometimes prefer to test new business models whose results may be known more quickly than innovations based on basic research—with the exception of a few fields such as quantum computing. And researchers don't care about basic research if they can quickly increase their standard of living significantly with a few operations closer to industry.

3.5 Financing Technology

China combines direct subventions, fiscal and taxation policies, banks, and capital markets. The first source of financing technology is public money. Most of the governmental programs listed in Chap. 2 were associated with sources of financing for technological innovation. This comes with tax advantages and includes exemption of import (and export) duties, reduction of the tax on benefit, and deductibility of R&D expenses. Public subsidies come also at the provincial, municipal, and district levels. Startups will be supported if they decide to settle in a science and technology park.

Banks support technology companies through lending. Yet, the traditional dominance of the state-owned banks which favor state-owned companies is a handicap for private companies—large and small. On top of this, because of their administrative origin, they do not take risks if they do not have solid guarantees.

Another option is venture capital and private equity investment. This goes mostly for startups with risky projects. Chinese companies raise funding not only from Chinese investors; venture capital companies in China are about 3500. They include foreign companies as well as Chinese companies. Among the largest ones, we have China Growth Capital, Shenzhen Capital Group, Suzhou Venture Group, UDG Capital, China Merchants Capital (subsidiary of China Merchants Group), GGV Capital, Mirae Assets China, China Renaissance, Sequoia Capital China, and Cowin Capital. These VCs cover the seed stage, mid-stage, late stage, and growth investment. Yet, the preferred model is the pre-IPO. The amounts raised have considerably increased since 2005. China became the first place in Asia for venture capital.

Chinese technology companies also access financing through the stock exchange. The first one was the ChiNext—launched on the Shenzhen Stock Exchange in 2009. More than 500 companies are listed on Chi Next. Two other options exist: the Star Market—launched in Shanghai in 2019 (see vignette), and the Beijing Stock Exchange—which reopened in 2021 (it was closed since 1952). This later will be dedicated to innovative SMEs, thus reproducing in Beijing the "Star Market" model set up in Shanghai. It could accommodate 200–300 introductions per year.

Vignette: The Star Market

The Star Market was launched in 2019 as a board of the Shanghai Stock Exchange. It is also known as the Science and Technology Innovation Board. It is dedicated to scientific and technological companies. The launch of the Star Market followed the creation of ChiNext (based in Shenzhen) and the New Third Board (NTB) compartment in 2013—all three launched with the same objective of enabling Chinese technology companies to access public savings (NTB has since fallen into oblivion). The Star Market is the third Chinese attempt in ten years. The rationale was for a more flexible regime. It is therefore not simply an answer to Americans. It is part of a long-term strategy. This creation is also linked to the "Made in China 2025" plan in the sense that the activities targeted by the Star Market largely overlap with those of the plan.

More generally, this launch consolidates China's position as a new player in technology creation. Star Market started with 25 companies listed from the biotech, semiconductors, information technologies, new materials, and new energies—not well known outside China; the bar of 300 companies was bypassed during the summer of 2021. The place is a Sino-Chinese one. The Star Market is for Chinese tech companies and Chinese investors. Foreigners who wanted to invest on the Shanghai Stock Exchange had to already obtain the status of Qualified Foreign Institutional Investor (QFII) in order to finally hold a total of less than 5% of the securities in the place. They will still have to wait to be accepted at the Star Market club. While there are 200 Chinese companies listed in the USA—including the famous Alibaba and Baidu on the NYSE—there will be no foreign company listed on Star Market. Once again, the question of reciprocity, or rather the absence of it, arises. And interestingly, the Chinese government targets the 100 million Chinese stock marketers since they are asked to have a low minimum portfolio (the equivalent of $70,000) and two years of trading experience.

3.6 An Increasing R&D Investment by Chinese and Foreign Firms

The Move Is Massive and Recent

Over the past 15 years, a growing number of companies, both public and private, both Chinese and foreign, have engaged in R&D in China. To position China's investment, Fig. 3.2 shows the R&D investment of leading countries.

In the group of the leading industrialized countries, China is the one which has accomplished the most important transformation in terms of real R&D spending: over 20 years, the total spending went from US$40

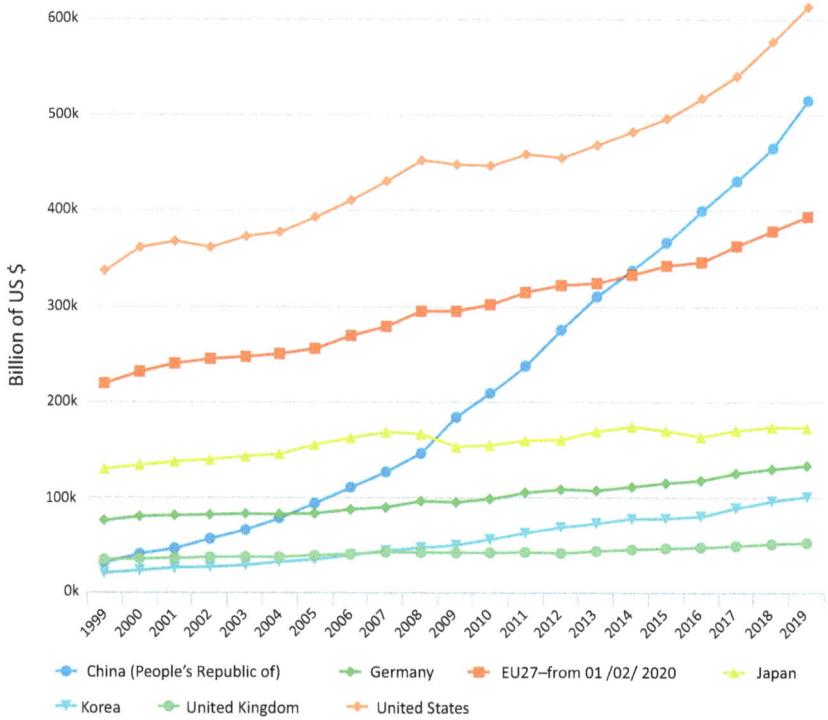

Fig. 3.2 Gross domestic spending on R&D. (Source: OECD)

billion (in 2000) to US$515 billion (in 2019). The annual investment was multiplied by 12.8! In the same period, all the other industrialized countries, that is, the UK, France, Germany, Japan, and the USA have also increased their R&D spending—but, by a factor less than 2—with the notable exceptions of South Korea and Taiwan. South Korea has multiplied its budget by 4 and Taiwan by 3.6. So, the USA is the only country in the world still spending more than China on R&D. Yet, on its current trajectory, China will overtake the USA within the next decade.

Investment in R&D in China is geographically very localized: Beijing, Shanghai, and the provinces of Guangdong, Zhejiang, Jiangsu, Shandong, and Hubei—and consequently again mainly on the coast. This geographical divide is not new. Authorities have put in place programs (like the "Go West Policy" of the former president Jiang Zemin), but there are still major discrepancies between the coast and the inner country. And this divide is not only for R&D investment. This is also true for top universities, patenting, inward foreign direct investment, and high GDP per capita—which are all concentrated on the coast.

Investment in R&D includes both companies manufacturing products (Huawei in the telephone equipment, BYD in electric cars, Sany in construction equipment, Haier in household appliances, or Avic in aeronautics) as well as companies which work in the intangible (such as Tencent, the world number two in instant messaging).

In terms of human resources, China had 4.4 million people working in R&D in 2018—including 1.9 million researchers. The challenge for China remains to transform these massive investments into innovative capacities.

China Devotes Less Resources to Fundamental Research Than Other Industrialized Countries

As mentioned earlier, investment in fundamental research is too limited to bring about new paradigms. Basic research represents 5% of budgets in China—compared to a share of 10–15% in OECD countries. The USA remains by far the largest investor in fundamental and applied research in the world. But, again, things are changing in China: the figure rose to 6% in 2019. And the 8% mark is in sight under the 14th five-year plan (2021–2025).

The fact that China is a new player in research appears in Table 3.6, which gives the number of researchers per 1000 inhabitants. China has moved from 1 to 3 researchers in a little bit more than a decade; yet, with 3 researchers per 1000 inhabitants, the country is last in this table. Compared with Taiwan and other small countries (in terms of the number of inhabitants) like the Scandinavian countries, the gap is huge. This emphasis made by Taiwan is one explanation of its leadership in semiconductors. Even with established industrialized countries (the USA, Japan, Germany, etc.)—which have about 10 researchers per 1000 inhabitants, the difference is still significant. Again, the high figure for South Korea (16) illustrates the importance of research for this country. But, those figures also mean that China has some slack and that if the country can foster the development of its universities, it has a huge reservoir to tap into.

Private Companies Are the Main Engine

State-owned companies like Petro-China, China Railway, and Aviation Industry Corporation of China (Avic) are serious R&D spenders. Yet, most of the investments come from private firms. Companies like Huawei and ZTE in telecommunications equipment, Mindray in medical equipment, Baidu, Alibaba, and Tencent in the Internet, BYD in automotive manufacturing, Trina Solar in photovoltaic panels, Haier and Hisense in home appliances, and even Sany in construction machinery, are emerging in their industries as champions of R&D investment. Mindray, for example, was established in 1991 in Shenzhen; the company announces that it devoted 10% of its turnover to R&D over the past ten years. Even in the insurance sector—which is, strictly speaking, not a high-tech industry, the insurance company Ping An devotes 1% of its turnover to R&D (for easy recognition, artificial intelligence in medical, traffic flow assessment, etc.), employs 24,000 people in R&D (out of a total of 326,000), and has a portfolio of 9500 patents.

3 The Chinese National System of Innovation 49

Table 3.6 Number of researchers per 1000 inhabitants

	China	Taiwan	USA	Japan	Germany	France	UK	S. Korea	Norway	Sweden	Denmark	Finland	Canada
2004	1	19	8	10	7	8	8	7	9	11	10	17	8
2005	1	20	8	10	7	8	9	8	9	13	10	16	8
2006	2	20	8	10	7	8	9	9	9	13	10	16	8
2007	2	20	8	10	7	8	9	9	10	10	10	15	9
2008	2	20	8	10	8	8	9	10	10	11	12	16	9
2009	2	21	9	10	8	9	9	10	10	11	13	16	9
2010	2	21	8	10	8	9	9	11	10	11	13	17	9
2011	2	22	9	10	8	9	9	12	11	11	14	16	9
2012	2	22	9	10	8	10	9	13	11	11	14	16	9
2013	2	22	9	10	8	10	9	13	11	14	14	15	9
2014	2	22	9	10	8	10	9	13	11	14	15	15	9
2015	2	22	9	10	9	10	9	14	11	14	15	15	9
2016	2	22	9	10	9	10	9	14	12	14	16	14	9
2017	2	23	9	10	9	11	9	14	12	15	15	14	9
2018	2	23	10	10	10	11	9	15	12	15	15	14	9
2019	3	23	10	10	10	11	10	16	13	15	15	15	9

Source: OECD, https://data.oecd.org/rd/researchers.htm

What Foreign Companies Can Do?

Companies like Ericsson or IBM have a long experience in doing R&D in China (von Zedtwitz, 2004). Companies from the pharmaceutical industry (Eli Lilly, Pfizer, GSK, etc.) have as well been doing some R&D—much more D than R. General Electric, General Motors, Nestlé, Bosch, and Microsoft have also created major R&D centers in China. In the 2009 Fortune 500 ranking, only 98 companies had an R&D center in China. The figure for foreign R&D centers climbed to 1600 in 2013 (according to KPMG), and has probably continued to increase. Some centers are really big, that is, employing several thousands of researchers. Why such keen interest?

Drivers for implementing an R&D center in China changed over time (Jolly et al., 2015, 2016). As shown in Fig. 3.3, starting with cost-driven R&D, companies moved to marketing-driven R&D, and are now targeting knowledge-driven R&D.

The first foreign companies to come to China to do R&D were initially motivated by cost advantages. As shown in Fig. 3.4, their activities were then concentrated in the most labor-intensive activities, and therefore at the end of development—keeping research activities on their national territory. Those cases were concentrated in industries requiring laborious testing operations—software and pharmaceuticals, for example. Ericsson, SAP, or Pfizer are good illustrations; those companies came

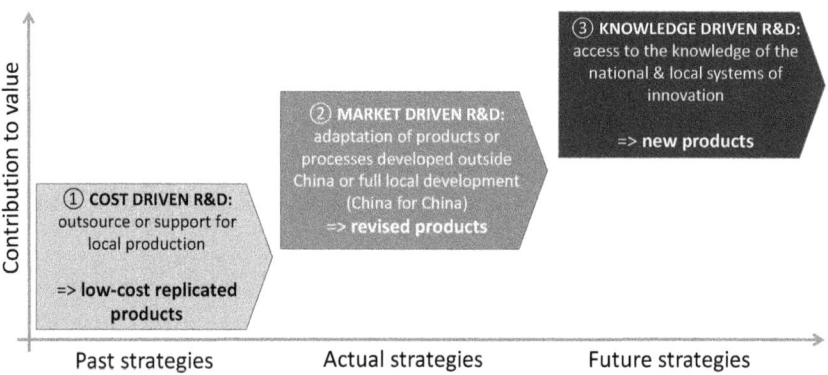

Fig. 3.3 Drivers for foreign R&D centers in China have changed

3 The Chinese National System of Innovation   51

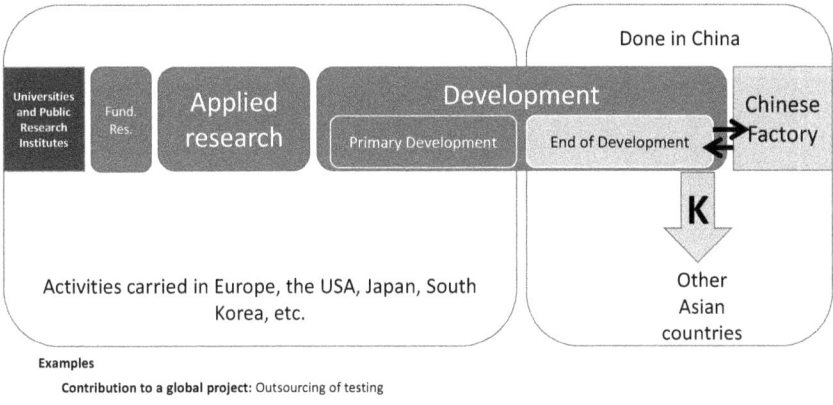

Examples
Contribution to a global project: Outsourcing of testing
Match with manufacturing: Small domestic appliances

Fig. 3.4 Cost-driven R&D: end of development

to China for the end of development, that is, essentially to conduct tests at a lower cost than in their home country. Most of the knowledge came from the headquarters in developed countries; little knowledge was developed in China. As labor costs go up, this driver has become less and less relevant—except for companies that have been deciding to locate their testing center in remote areas where labor costs are still low.

As their Chinese R&D centers matured and the Chinese market has grown, vernacular forces gained momentum, but labor prices have continued to increase. As shown in Fig. 3.5, foreigners broadened the scope of their activities to include all product development operations: end of development and primary development. The goal of reducing R&D costs has become less important. As technologies developed in the West have not always fitted to China's domestic conditions, it has become more of a question of setting up an R&D unit to localize technologies. This means adapting technologies initially developed by foreign companies on their national territory to the Chinese market to meet local demand, to co-create with customers, to adjust to local resources, and to comply with local standards and regulations. This cannot be done remotely. This strategy was initially most prevalent in industries such as autos, food, cosmetics, and construction materials. For example, the cream developed by L'Oréal to reduce wrinkles does not suit the Chinese population where aging comes with spots (rather than wrinkles). Car manufacturers had

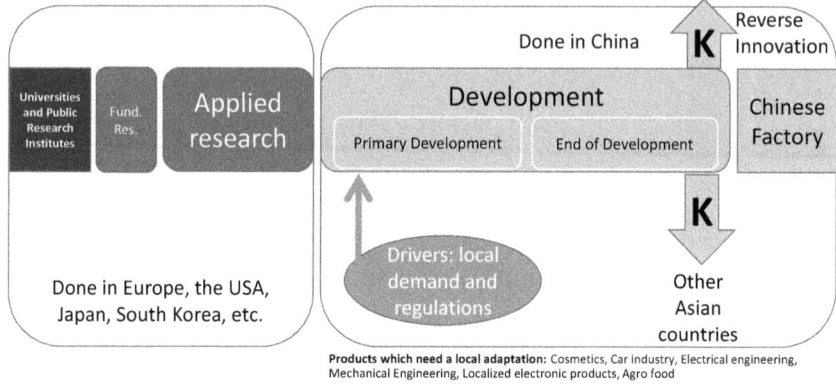

Fig. 3.5 Marketing-driven R&D: focus on development

also frequently to redesign their models with a sedan trunk or to stretch their premium models to increase comfort of people sitting in the back as they can afford to have a driver.

The last step, currently underway, started in the mid- to late 2000s. It is based on the fundamental transformation affecting the Chinese national innovation system; it is gradually becoming a place of technological creation. Consequently, a growing number of foreign firms—such as Microsoft, Philips, General Electric, Novartis, Astra Zeneca, or Solvay—come to seek, not low wages, not to fit the market, but to match with Chinese scientists engaged in research, who make inventions, who offer innovations. Figure 3.6 illustrates this comprehensive option. This driver is becoming the most important driver for foreign companies willing to set up an R&D center in China. With this option where the Chinese unit becomes the focal point for the world, business units need to gain the support of their headquarters. This option allows locally developed knowledge to be transferred to other company locations for worldwide use. A downside: a 2018 law requires foreign companies to seek permission from Chinese authorities to transfer out of China the results of their R&D that has been carried out in China.

Challenges to Foreign Companies

The establishment of R&D activities in China poses at least two managerial challenges. The first relates to the location of activities and its interactions with its milieu. Cost-driven R&D has had to follow the manufacturing sector into China's interior, where costs are lower than in coastal regions. There is a need for a high degree of connection between R&D and production; units need to be close to Chinese factories to provide technical assistance. Market-driven R&D needs to be close to where the customers are. There is no need to be based in an S&T park. For example, automakers' equipment suppliers need their R&D centers to be located near the automakers' factories, which are scattered across the country. Knowledge-driven R&D, in contrast, needs to be conducted close to research universities and public research institutes. Locations should facilitate access to local systems of innovation (LSI) and/or the national system of innovation (NSI). These are predominantly established in the coastal provinces—in first-tier cities, but also in second-tier cities such as Hangzhou, Nanjing, and Suzhou. A company pursuing knowledge-driven R&D will therefore typically need to open a new facility. Fortunately, MNCs can often receive incentives from provincial or municipal governments eager to attract investment and create jobs.

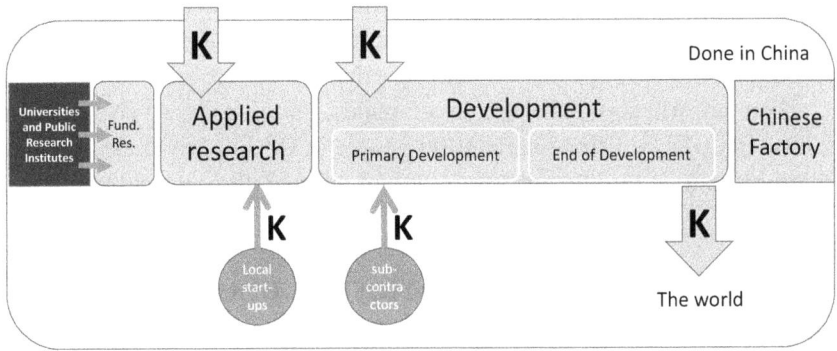

Fig. 3.6 Knowledge-driven R&D: the full R&D spectrum

The second challenge relates to personnel management and organizational settings. For market-driven R&D, you need to hire R&D managers with marketing sensibility. For knowledge-driven R&D, you need to recruit good scientists (with a higher proportion of PhD degrees than other modes, and more returnees). Developing creativity in a culture where education is primarily based on repetition, where the debate of ideas has little room, and where the hierarchy makes it impossible to challenge established positions, is a challenge. If the Chinese are successful in sports—as evidenced by the collection of medals collected at the Olympic Games—it is precisely because success in sporting events requires relentless repetition of the same gesture. On the contrary, innovators are always exploring alternative avenues and are not afraid of failure. Innovation is not part of the mainstream mindset. It requires confrontation—hardly compatible with Confucian culture. If there is only one Chinese Nobel Prize in science, there are many scientists of Chinese origin in the USA who are very successful—which proves that the problem lies primarily in education and in the work context. In addition, political blockage also works against innovation; in a society where political power is not criticized, individuals withdraw into themselves. Innovation requires a climate of freedom that is not distinctive to the current Chinese regime. The technical competence of the people hired is usually not a problem. On the other hand, the management of a young staff, with little experience, weakly inclined to creativity and to taking initiatives and responsibilities, but committed, responsive, dynamic, and in great demand by the market, among other things, requires a lot of skill.

There are still some changes in strategies. Oracle reduced the wing in China in 2019 by firing nearly 1000 people in R&D both in Beijing and in Shenzhen; its Beijing R&D center had opened 20 years earlier.

3.7 A Protecting Regulatory Framework

China acceded in 1980 to the World Intellectual Property Office (WIPO), joined the Paris Convention in 1985, and signed the Washington Treaty of 1994 for cooperation in patent matters, among other things. As can be seen from Table 3.7, China has acceded to many conventions and passed many laws. China ratified several international conventions early on.

Table 3.7 Chinese regulation framework

Year	Adhesions/laws
1980	World Industrial Property Office (WIPO)
1985	Paris Union Convention for the Protection of Industrial Property
1989	Madrid Settlement in International Registrations of Brands
1991	Software Protection Decree
1992	Berne Convention for the Protection of Literary and Artistic Works
1993	Geneva Convention for the Protection of Producers of Phonogram
1994	Washington Treaty for Patent Cooperation
2000	Revision of 1984 Law on Patents
2001	Revision of 1982 Law on Brands
2001	Revision of 1990 Law on Copyrights

Chinese domestic law is therefore now considered to be part of several international conventions on patents, trademarks, and copyright. China's entry into the WTO (2001) has been accompanied by actions by the Chinese government aimed at reducing intellectual property violations. For example, there are Chinese rules (both nationally and provincially) on the remuneration for inventors. There are also avenues of action for infringement (administrative, civil, criminal, and customs). Yet, the practice of copying foreign technologies has not been eradicated.

3.8 Conclusion

This chapter has shown that China had put in place, step by step, all the different components necessary to have a national system of innovation. Figure 3.7 offers an integrated perspective to the guidance run by the government and the role of the different stakeholders. Research in universities and public research centers took off in terms of publishing of scientific articles as well as spin-offs of startups, and the unicorns which emerged. An increasing number of companies with very different profiles devote resources to R&D. They found in the numerous science and technology parks optimal locations to run those activities so as to be in a symbiotic relationship with other actors of innovation. They are also supported by several financial stakeholders. In addition, innovators are now protected by a recognized regulatory framework.

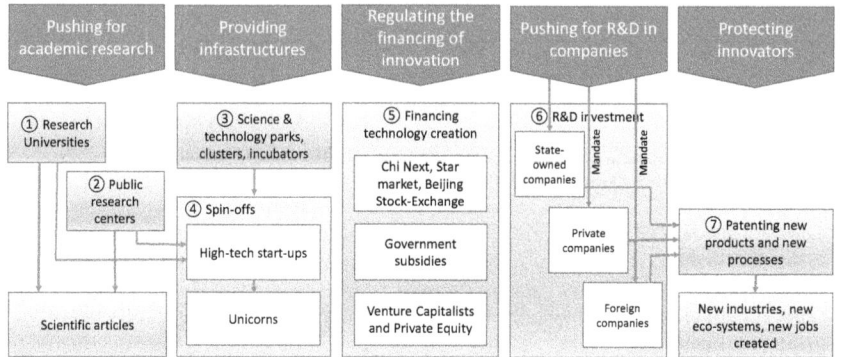

Fig. 3.7 The Chinese government as a conductor and its performers for technology creation

The emergence of the Chinese National System of Innovation developed much faster by bundling those components as did other countries such as India, Indonesia, or Brazil. The machine has been launched; with the exception of societal tensions, upheavals, and/or political conflicts, it should continue to run. China is now on the world R&D map. Let's look more closely at the situation in different industries.

References

Jolly, D., & Masetti, F. (2016). The winding path for foreign companies: Building R&D Centers in China. *The Journal of Business Strategy, 37*(2), 3–11.

Jolly, D., McKern, B., & Yip George, S. (2015). The next innovation opportunity in China. Multinationals are shifting their R&D focus from cost savings to knowledge-based research. *Strategy+Business*, issue 80, 16–19.

Jolly, D., Yip George, S., & McKern, B. (2016). Multinational corporations' innovation in China. In S. Yip George & B. McKern (Eds.), *China's next strategic advantage – from imitation to innovation* (pp. 101–127). The MIT Press. isbn: 978-0-262-03458-6.

Jolly, D., & Zhu, F. (2012). Chinese S&T parks: A news model is emerging. *The Journal of Business Strategy, 33*(5), 4–13.

Nelson, R. R. (1993). *National innovation systems – A comparative analysis*. Oxford University Press.

Nelson, R., & Rosenberg, N. (1993). Technical innovation and national systems. In *National innovation systems – A comparative analysis*. Oxford University Press, pp. 3–21.

Petti, C., & Ederer, M. (2012). *Technological entrepreneurship in China: How does it work?* Edward Elgar Publishing.

Shan, J., & Jolly, D. (2011). Patterns of technological learning and catch-up strategies in latecomer firm: Case study in China's telecom-equipment industry. *Journal of Technology Management in China, 6*(2), 153–170.

Shan, J., & Jolly, D. (2013). Technological innovation capabilities, product strategy, and firm performance: The electronics industry in China. *Canadian Journal of Administrative Sciences/Revue canadienne des sciences de l'administration, 30*(3), 159–172.

von Zedtwitz, M. (2004). Managing foreign R&D laboratories in China. *R&D Management, 34*(4), 439–452.

4

The Iconic Case of Telecommunications

Abstract The Chinese telecommunication industry is made up of three different actors: (1) the equipment suppliers—a global B2B oligopoly driven by technological innovation; (2) the smartphone producers—a B2C fringed oligopoly, also global and technology driven; and (3) the operators—exclusively local and incredibly concentrated with only three firms for 1.4 billion citizens. The study of the three leading actors in each segment—Huawei, Xiaomi, and China Mobile—reveals impressive development paths. This can be explained by three factors: (a) using the impetus given by foreign companies to access technology, Chinese companies have then built their own innovative capabilities; (b) firms have access to a massive market which helped to amplify scale effects; (c) there is in China a symbiotic relationship between economic actors and political decision-makers; this porosity has a cost when it comes to international development, as it's a source of fear for non-Chinese customers.

Keywords 5G • Technology-driven • Scale effects • Political issues

The telecommunication industry covers three different stages: the handsets, the equipment, and the operators. The handsets business is a B2C sector. The equipment is a B2B sector; it's about what happens between two smartphones, that is, hardware and software, which consumers do not see. This includes routers, switches, base stations, cell towers, associated software, and submarine cables. And operators buy those devices from equipment suppliers to offer services to their subscribers. Figure 4.1 depicts the situation in China.

The industry is emblematic because the main actors for hardware—Huawei and Xiaomi—have been successful not only in China but also outside China. They embodied the threat to the USA (Allison et al., 2021). This international development of those companies has been much stronger than the one of Chinese Internet companies, which are still primarily based in China. In this chapter, I examine the case of Huawei which is covering the first two stages, and the case of Xiaomi which started with handsets, and finally China Mobile—which is the first operator in China. Each of those businesses are very specific in China. First, operators are incredibly concentrated: only three companies for 1.4 billion people. The smartphone industry is also fascinating. Xiaomi did not exist in 2009, and it is now the first one of the business. Finally, in the equipment business, the development path of Huawei is as much impressive. This case is one aspect of the competition between China and the USA—a competition which has no precedent in history! The common thread to those three businesses of the telecommunication industry is the tremendous impact of the Chinese government and the role of political forces.

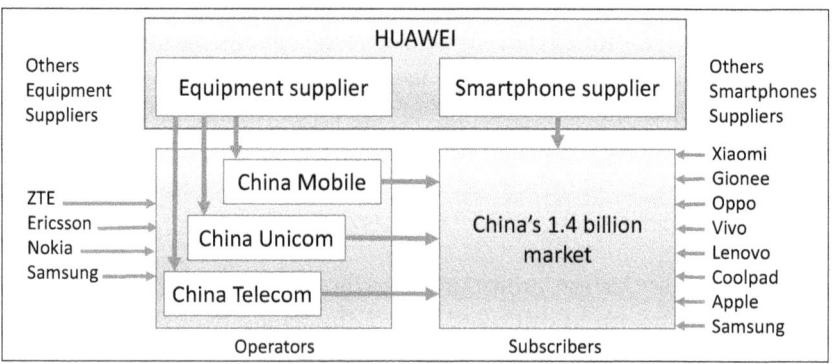

Fig. 4.1 China's telecommunication industry

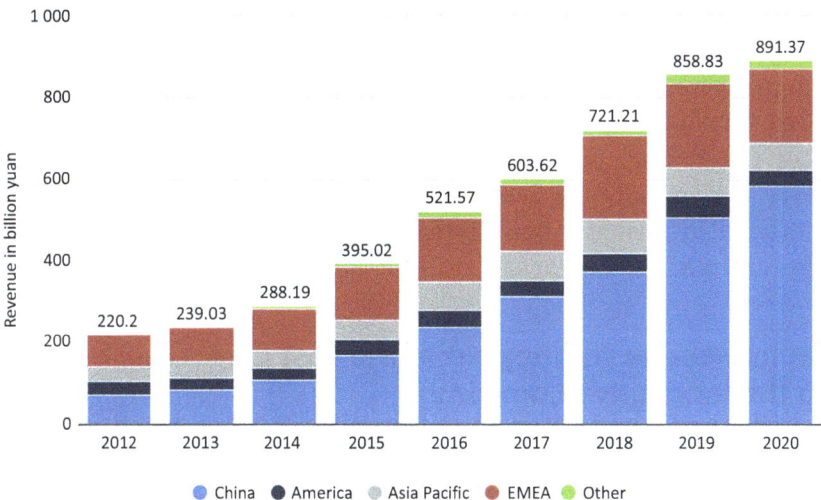

Fig. 4.2 Huawei revenue from 2012 to 2020, by geographical region

4.1 Huawei: Only Technological Advantages?

Huawei is unarguably, along with Alibaba, the most well-known Chinese company outside of China. Several authors have studied the case (see, e.g., Tian & Wu, 2015; Haour & von Zedtwitz, 2016; Guo et al., 2019). It is one of the few truly globalized Chinese firms, with a commercial presence in more than 170 countries. Figure 4.2 depicts Huawei revenue outside China.

It has been in the Fortune 500 ranking since 2010. The company has experienced impressive growth. While the revenue was less than a billion in 1997, it bypassed $100 Billion in 2018 (with a profit of 8.7 billion). The firm is known to the general public for its smartphones. But its historical business is the telephone equipment (like Ericsson or Nokia).

A Private or a Public Company?

Huawei employed 190,000 people in 2021—including 70,000 Chinese employees who would hold more than 90% of the company's capital via a trade union committee since it is a workers' cooperative (this original statute was born in 1980 in Shenzhen; it disappeared shortly after). Internal governance procedures are not known to the public. However, given the power of unions in China, some have suggested that this would make the company public even if it claims to be private. No less than 7% of the staff are said to be members of the Chinese Communist Party. The founder Ren Zhengfei, born in the poor province of Guizhou in 1944 (78 years old in 2022), holds 1% of the capital.

An Impressive Journey: From the Lost Cost to the Innovative Company

Huawei started in Shenzhen in 1987 as a supplier of telephone equipment to China. The beginnings were made by targeting small towns and rural areas that foreign manufacturers had abandoned. Once installed in China, the firm led from 1997 an international strategy targeting again the territories where Westerners did not want to go. Huawei has most likely received official backing in its international development—even though the company is deemed private. In 2004, with a turnover of $3.8 billion, Huawei was only one-sixth of the then leader, Ericsson. By targeting easy-to-reach countries, Huawei has built a market base focusing on cost (Zeng & Williamson, 2007). It was only after that the company gradually attacked developed countries. It now supplies leading operators such as Orange, Vodafone, British Telecom, Deutsche Telecoms, and Telefonica. Huawei became, in 2010, the world number two in telephone equipment behind Ericsson.

Since 2017, Huawei has the largest share of the global infrastructure market: 28%. Ericsson owns 27%, Nokia 23%, ZTE 13%, and several small players—including Samsung—hold the remainder, 9% (former American national champions Lucent and Motorola crashed). The Vietnamese authorities which have made the unusual choice of a national supplier, the company Viettel, find themselves sixth in the race. Huawei invests considerable sums in R&D; more than 50,000 people would work in R&D. They are mainly located in China, but are also present abroad (including Sweden, the USA, India, Indonesia, Russia, Ireland, the UK, Italy, and France). R&D spending would have reached nearly $14 billion in 2017, or 15% of sales. Huawei would hold no less than 87,000 patents; the company filed 5400 international applications in 2018 and 4400 in 2019.

The Denial of the USA

Huawei started its research on 5G infrastructures in 2009. The three Chinese operators (China Mobile, China Unicom, and China Telecom) started to implement 5G in 2019; China could have 600 million 5G subscribers by 2025 (while Europe lags behind in deployment). Chinese operators implemented 1.2 million 5G base stations at the end of 2021, and plan to have 3.64 million at the end of 2025 (China Daily). In this Chinese market, Huawei will grab the essentials; foreigners will only get a few crumbs. Outside of China, Huawei is looking to license its 5G technology to telecommunication companies.

The company remains virtually absent from the USA or Australia regarding equipment supply. In fact, Huawei concentrates everything that scares US authorities. US officials have many doubts about the company. They are suspicious because Ren Zhengfei, the founding boss, is both a member of the Chinese Communist Party and a former Chinese military official (from which he graduated in 1982); they suspect him of being the armed wing of the Chinese economic intelligence. They refuse to entrust even a small part of their mobile telecommunications system (and in particular the routers which constitute its core) to a company potentially linked to Chinese power. Huawei is therefore excluded from tenders for national security reasons. It was also prevented from making acquisitions of American firms. In China, on the contrary, Ren Zhengfei became a living legend; he is the embodiment of Chinese economic and technological success.

But American authorities don't hear it that way. Investing in 5G networks developed by Huawei would be a nightmare for them. They assert that the Chinese government will use Huawei to spy on client countries or launch silent cyber-attacks: it is the fear of a Chinese backdoor into Western networks. How Huawei might use the colossal amount of data collected is a legitimate question. And given the opacity, the porosity between public and private, the practices of monitoring populations, and the treatment of human rights that prevail in China, we have serious doubts! What proves that the data collected will not be used by the Chinese government for geopolitical purposes? The power horizons opened up by 5G—the communication between billions of connected objects (susceptible to be attacked)—mean that all countries will want to be perfectly sure of their suppliers. No one wants his telecommunication content to be intercepted. No ruler wants a foreigner to be able to interfere with their critical infrastructure networks: water, electricity, the Internet, hospitals, traffic lights, train networks, airports, and so forth.

Ren Zhengfei's disclaimers did not change anything. Americans are probably not wrong to be cautious of Huawei. Chinese law allows the government to order a Chinese company to deliver customer data to it. In view of the investments made by Beijing in the internal security of the country, one can imagine that the Chinese authorities have the same intelligence service for the world.

The Refusal to Open Up to Chinese 5G Extended Beyond the USA

Australia, New Zealand, and Japan are like the USA opposed to Huawei's 5G deployment. India has threatened to ban Huawei. In Europe, the UK has placed restrictions on Huawei by allowing Vodafone and its competitors to purchase peripheral hardware (such as antennas and base stations) but not key hardware. The British have also capped Huawei's share at 35% of the market. In Sweden, Ericsson's homeland, Huawei and ZTE have been banned by the government from bidding. Other European countries, such as the Czech Republic and Slovenia have also banned Huawei.

If the USA lost the battle for 5G, they intend to catch up with the next generation. Industry players have started to network in anticipation of 6G. This should make it possible to further reduce latency and provide increased power for the benefit of health, driverless cars, artificial intelligence, and financial markets, among others. It will open up perspectives in the Internet of Senses and the Internet of Behavior. It should be effective before 2030. Chinese companies like Huawei and Unicom have also been active in 6G since 2018.

The Daughter of the Founder Under House Arrest in Canada

It is in this context that Ren Zhengfei's daughter, Meng Wanzhou, who is also the group's financial director, was arrested in Vancouver (Canada) in December 2018 on a request from the USA, which suspects the Huawei group of selling to Iran products incorporating American components. Meng Wanzhou was kept under house arrest with the threat of being extradited to the USA. Her lawyers have been busy and questioned the extradition. Since the arrest, diplomatic relations between Beijing and Ottawa have been freezing. In May 2020, Canada confirmed its lawsuits. Chinese retaliation with the accusation of espionage brought by Beijing against two Canadian citizens (condemned during summer 2021) and the embargo on several agricultural products imported from Canada (such as canola) were not enough to get out of the status quo. Meng was finally liberated in September 2021 as the US authorities agreed to differ their pursuits, and the two Canadian citizens were as well liberated.

The US Threat to Supplies Seriously Impacted Huawei

Huawei purchased $11 billion worth of components and services from more than 1000 US companies in 2018. Specifically, for 5G, Huawei must source semiconductors from the US companies Broadcom, Xilinx, Texas Instruments, and Analog Devices. De-americanization is a wise choice as the USA was able to put Huawei's competitor ZTE in difficulty by refusing to deliver processors to it. Huawei was also prevented from sourcing components from American suppliers before President Trump reversed his decision (the move also means lower turnover for American companies). Huawei could be in trouble when it comes to key components.

The US threat was used by Ren Zhengfei to convince his teams that the solution lies in internal development. Huawei has its own semiconductor design center, Hi Silicon, with 10,000 people. This unit designed the Kirin chips. But it has to outsource manufacturing to Taiwanese TSMC and American Micron; 5G is a real opportunity for these two suppliers. In the event of a break with the USA, Huawei could always call on the Korean SK Hynix. With its decisions targeting Huawei, the Trump administration may well change the face of telecommunications in the future.

Forward Vertical Integration in Smartphones

Huawei has also grown significantly in smartphones, which now represent one-third of its turnover. The business was launched in 2003. In 2011, Huawei only sold 1 million phones. The figure rose to 75 million phones in 2014. The 100 million bar was passed in 2015. In 2016, the figure jumped to 139 million. And the 200 million was reached in 2018. It was his Ascend smartphone that made Huawei known to the general public. Huawei is in direct competition with Apple and Samsung (declining in China). As shown in Table 4.1, the year 2019 went even better. Although it has become the third largest smartphone maker in the world, the gap with Samsung remains marked.

Huawei's strategy in smartphones is clear: move upmarket. Huawei is therefore developing its own processors and sourcing optics from Leica. The manufacturer brought a 5G smartphone to the market in 2019—the Mate X with a fold-out screen at 2300 euros ($ 2600). The challenge lies in the operating system. Huawei uses Google's Android operating system.

Table 4.1 Smartphones sold per year worldwide (in million)

	World	Samsung	Apple	Huawei	Xiaomi
2013	1.014	316	153	48	19
2014	1.294	315	192	75	60
2015	1.430	325	231	105	78
2016	1.470	306	215	139	Not available
2017	1.465	317	216	152	90
2018	1.405	290	208	205	123
2019	1.371	295	191	241	123
2020	1.294	267	207	189	148
2021	1.355	272	236	35	191

Source: IDC

But the threat of a US refusal to continue supplying Huawei looms large. The company certainly has internally with the Hongmeng platform a substitute for Android and with Harmony an evolution of Android. Knowing that Huawei makes 50% of its turnover with the phone, tablets, and laptops, the launch of its own operating system (an idea on which Nokia, BlackBerry, Microsoft, Intel, Palm, Firefox, Samsung, and Jolla, all broke their teeth) would be a serious handicap outside of China. It is indeed difficult for consumers to quit the Google ecosystem to which they are accustomed. This is why losing access to Android could become a major handicap for Huawei outside of China. As a matter of fact, sales of smartphones started to tumble in 2020 (see Table 4.1). Because of US sanctions, Huawei shipments for 2021 went down by 82% to 35 million units; yet, it's former brand Honor sold 40 million units.

The Diversification Strategy

Huawei has been offering its own payment system since 2015, developed with China Union Pay, in a market dominated by Alibaba and Tencent. The company also offers cloud services (again competing with Alibaba and Tencent). An agreement has been made with Microsoft which will provide applications on Huawei's cloud. The group is as well engaged in research on 5G-based telecommunications systems for assisted driving. It also entered the business of connected watches. It is investing in artificial intelligence and speech recognition. Irony of the trade war between China and the USA: absent from the USA, Huawei does not have to suffer the impact of the taxes which American buyers of iPhone will take full force.

4.2 Xiaomi: A Dramatic Growth

A Serial Entrepreneur

Xiaomi is a private company. It was created in 2010 in Beijing by the charismatic Lei Jun (53 years old in 2022), an Internet pioneer in China, a clone of Steve Jobs, who was not at his first entrepreneurial attempt.

He first worked for Kingsoft—a software company—after graduating from college in 1992. He ran Shunwei Capital, a venture capital fund, and started multiple companies. He made his first coup in 2004 by selling the online bookstore Joyo.com he had founded four years earlier to Amazon for $75 million. When Xiaomi was created, Lei Jun gathered around him an experienced team, many of whom traveled to the USA and worked for the US majors (Microsoft, Oracle, Google, Motorola, etc.). He was backed up by several investment companies, including Temasek.

The Company Experienced Dramatic Growth

Xiaomi released a wide range of smartphones on the Chinese market using its operation system MIUI based on Google's Android operating system (thus creating a dependence on the American while Apple controls its software and hardware). The company is using semiconductors from Qualcomm. Seven million smartphones were sold in 2012; almost 19 million in 2013. The figure reached 60 million in 2014 and the turnover reached $12 billion. It rose to 78 million in 2015—including 65 million in China—123 million in 2018, and 148 in 2020 (cf. Table 4.1).

Xiaomi stole the crown in China from Samsung in 2014, overtaking established Chinese players like Huawei, Lenovo, or ZTE and crushing other lesser-known Chinese producers like Oppo, Vivo, Coolpad, or Gionee (who count their annual production in tens of millions). In 2015, Xiaomi would have taken 15% of the Chinese market ahead of Huawei and Apple even as the Chinese smartphone market is heading straight toward saturation. The startup was valued at $4 billion three years after its creation, and even $40 billion, four years after its creation. At the end of 2014, the workforce reached 7000 people. It exceeded 14,000 in 2017. The 20,000 were surpassed in 2020. In 2019, nine years after its creation, Xiaomi entered the Fortune Global 500 ranking. The revenue reached $38 billion in 2020.

The Cooperation with the Chinese Communist Party

Xiaomi is an emerging champion who seems to have needed no state support to take off. But, unsurprisingly, Lei Jun is a member of the Chinese Communist Party, a member of the Twelfth Chinese People's Political Consultative Conference, and one of Beijing's representatives in the National People's Congress. He is also vice-chairman of the All-China Federation of Industry and Commerce, an entity responsible for linking business and the Chinese Communist Party. Lei Jun's personal fortune exceeds $10 billion.

A Disruptive Strategy

Part of Xiaomi's success has been the opportunity for Chinese consumers to express their nationalism while achieving a good financial deal. But, that's not all. Xiaomi built its success on the trivialization of the smartphone in the largest market in the world: 920 million in China, 439 in India, 270 in the USA, 160 in Indonesia, 109 in Brazil, and 100 in Russia (source: Newzoo.com). The company is driven by un-refrained use of the smartphone, surpassing the use of the PC (since 2014, there are more Internet users in China via mobile than Internet users connected via a desktop computer). Xiaomi tackles the lower and middle levels of the income pyramid. These are therefore low-cost products. They are considered by Apple to be clones of its products. Foxconn is in charge of production. Xiaomi's smartphones are rated as good quality. In its early days, all products were sold on the Internet, via Weibo, WeChat, Baidu Tiebo, Xiaomi mall, and more, that is, where the young people are. The company has no sales force and little spending on advertising. Effective use of social media gives Xiaomi great hype and significant savings on the distribution business. Recently, the products are also available in stores (which would achieve at least 30% of sales). Another point is that the company is continuously updating its products; these continuous improvements are based on feedback received from customers. The company files more and more patents (mainly in China): 2300 in 2014, and 3600 in 2015. In 2020, its portfolio reached 28,000 patents. Ironically, Xiaomi has seen copies of its products appearing on the Chinese market.

Emergent Countries Have Preceded Developed Countries

In 2013, the company hired Hugo Barra, one of the bosses of the Android management team at Google, to develop international activities. He stayed until 2017. In 2014, Xiaomi's market was still 97% Chinese. Xiaomi began by entering the Indian market, then targeted Latin America by starting with Brazil, and attacked the African continent, that is, emerging countries where the company is looking for growth drivers. Intellectual property disputes are less likely there than they could be in the USA or Europe (Xiaomi, however, faces a legal attack from Ericsson on the Indian territory). In 2017, the share of its turnover outside China reached 28%. In 2020, it went to 50% (122.4/245.9 billion yuan). It will then be the turn of Russia, then Europe. And Xiaomi is even trying the USA from 2018. In 2021, Xiaomi reached the third place after Samsung and Apple, but before Huawei. And Xiaomi became the first market share in Europe in 2021.

The IOT Diversification

In the merciless world of mobile telephony, the top management of Xiaomi has undoubtedly kept in mind the case of HTC, the Taiwanese manufacturer of smartphones, which rose to the sky in the 2000s, was considered as the strongest rival to Apple, and descended into hell since 2011.[1] They must in particular face the proven shortage of the smartphone market in China and even around the world. The sector has indeed reached maturity: the number of smartphones sold even fell between 2017 and 2018 (from 1.5 billion to 1.4 billion units). Lei Jun doesn't want to make money on the hardware. He is much more aimed at a means of building a customer base to whom he can sell Internet services and accumulate data (which may one day be able to feed the generalized surveillance system that is Social Credit—see Chap. 8). Lei Jun talks about "triathlon": software, hardware, and internet services.

---

[1] The business was sold to Google in 2017.

Xiaomi dreams of founding its own ecosystem; this is why the company began, in 2014, to develop and market its own television. New products include white goods (pressure cooker, hair dryer, air purifier, fan, etc.) and even scooters.

Xiaomi bought in 2014 its first startup in the USA; this is Misfit, an Internet of Things player that produces "activity trackers." Xiaomi has acquired patents owned by Microsoft, Philips, and Nokia. In 2017, Xiaomi even released its own processor in an attempt to get rid of Qualcomm's domination. Xiaomi has entered into partnerships with a large network of startups that have agreed to join the Xiaomi ecosystem, four of which have become unicorns (ZMI, Huami, Ninebot, and Smart mi).

4.3 China Mobile: One Billion Subscribers

The company is the world's largest mobile phone operator with close to one billion subscribers. China Mobile overwhelmingly dominates its only two competitors, China Unicom and China Telecom, which have 324 and 242 million subscribers, respectively (in 2018). With China Mobile at 61% and its two competitors at 22% and 16%, the Chinese telecommunications services market is incredibly concentrated: the Herfindahl industry concentration index (sum of the square of market shares) is close to 0.50.

The company employs more than 200,000 people. It occupies all market segments. It operates within a gigantic ecosystem with the blessing of the Chinese state. The company is admittedly listed in New York and Hong Kong, but it remains 74% owned by the Chinese state. China Mobile has deployed in the past a Chinese 3G system called TD-SCDMA. It has put in place infrastructures for 5G with the help of Huawei and ZTE (i.e., without Ericsson and Nokia). Commercialization of 5G services started in 2019. The 100 million of 5G subscribers was reached in 2020 (including 70 million for China Mobile).

It is highly decentralized; the subsidiaries in the provinces are all responsible for their own income statement. China Mobile is mainly active in China alone. The only two exceptions are the takeover of Paktel, the Pakistani mobile operator in 2007 and the acquisition of an 18% stake in the capital of the Thai operator True Corporation in 2014 (third in his country).

4.4 Conclusion

The iconic case of the booming Chinese telecommunication industry shows that companies undertook strategies combining different aspects:

- Looking for government support. Operators being fully under state control, equipment suppliers and smartphones suppliers need to match with authorities.
- Learning from foreign competitors either through joint-ventures, hiring of returnees, hiring of foreign personnel, or even acquisitions.
- Investing strongly in R&D through in-house R&D and all other traditional means of access to forge significant patent portfolios. That's an impressive feature as most of those companies grounded initially their competitive advantage in low costs.
- Benefiting from a massive market acting as an amplifier and allowing the efficient exploitation of scale effects—a situation exemplified by China Mobile.

Those rules align with the LLL model suggested by Mathews (2006): learning (here from the West), leverage (here from the market), and linkage (here with the authorities). Yet, there are some clouds in the sky:

- Firms of the Chinese telecommunication industry still depend heavily on US suppliers not only for hardware but also for software. That's why one of the two major objectives of the latest (14th) five-year plan (2021–2025) is precisely technological autonomy.
- The telecommunication industry in China is moving toward maturity. And the next step is still unclear. Those telecommunication companies have the potential to become data companies—but this might be difficult to implement outside China. While they easily surfed on the growth phase, they will now have to move to maturity.

– Hardware producers (equipment and smartphones) expanded considerably outside China, while telecommunication operators have not really been able to significantly go beyond their China base.

References

Allison, G., Klyman, K., Barbesino, K., & Hugo, Y. (2021). *The great tech rivalry: China vs the U.S.* (p. 52).

Guo, L., Zhang, Y. M., Dodgson, M., Gann, D., & Hong, C. (2019). Seizing windows of opportunity by using technology-building and market-seeking strategies in tandem: Huawei's sustained catch-up in the global market. *Asia Pacific Journal of Management, 36*, 849–879.

Haour, G., & von Zedtwitz, M. (2016). *Created in China: How China is becoming a global innovator.* Bloomsbury.

Mathews, J. (2006). Dragon multinationals: New players in 21st century globalization. *Asia Pacific Journal of Management, 23*(1), 5–27.

Tian, T., & Wu, C. (2015). *The Huawei story.* Sage Publications.

Zeng, M., & Williamson, P. J. (2007). *Dragons at your door: How Chinese cost innovation is disrupting global competition.* Harvard Business School Press.

5

Companies of the Chinese Internet: The Only Potential Rival to Silicon Valley

Abstract Part of the success of the Chinese internet companies is due to the newness of the industry—they did not suffer strong disadvantages like companies in mature industries. Contrary to Huawei and Xiaomi, they do a large part of their business in China; they failed to internationalize their customers' bases—except those pursuing a focalization strategy like Didi or TikTok. They are all private, and foreign shareholders played an important role in their equity. They gain access to technology through means comparable to any Western company: in-house R&D, hiring specialists, and acquisition of startups. Again, those companies benefited from a huge mass market, exhibiting impressive numbers of active users, and this came with high companies' valuations. Again, they demonstrate how dependent they are on political bodies: alignment with authorities' expectations is compelling.

Keywords Emerging industry • Diversification strategies • Big data • Foreign shareholders • Scale effects • Connections with public authorities

Table 5.1 Largest Chinese companies by market capitalizations (end of 2021)

1	**Tencent**	596	11	Bank of China	140
2	Kweichou Moutai	382	12	Ping An	140
3	**Alibaba**	374	13	Wuliangye Yibin	136
4	ICBC	242	14	BYD	136
5	CATL	240	15	Petro China	136
6	**Meituan**	212	16	China Mobile	125
7	CM Bank	203	17	China Life Insurance	110
8	China Construction Bank	168	18	**Pinduoduo**	99
9	Agricultural Bank of China	156	19	**NetEase**	78
10	**Jingdong Mall**	147	20	Longi Green Energy	77

Source: https://companiesmarketcap.com/china/largest-companies-in-china-by-market-cap/

In public transport, it is becoming increasingly difficult to find someone in Shanghai who is not staring at his smartphone. People don't look at each other anymore; they don't talk to each other—they're online. The youngest are on games—the Tencent "Honor of Kings"—has 350 million registered users in China and about 100 million daily active users. Adults are on their email, watching a movie, series, or TV show. Others shop on Jingdong.com, others surf, and others read.

On the street, the great days of hailing taxis are over; everything now happens through the Didi reservation center—the Chinese Uber. As always, China stuns us with its numbers. The value of Didi—a company founded in 2012—has exceeded $40 billion. And the company continues to build an ecosystem around the automobile. At the end of 2021, as shown in Table 5.1, among the 20 top market capitalizations[1] in China, there are 6 Internet companies (see gray cells).

With all the actors and the technological resources described in Chap. 3, China has founded its own powerful digital ecosystem (McKinsey Global Institute, 2017; Kim & Chen, 2018; Jolly, 2021). The USA has the GAFAM: Google, Amazon, Facebook, Apple, and Microsoft. China has the BATX: Baidu, Alibaba, Tencent, and Xiaomi. Their profiles are depicted in Table 5.2.

How different are they? This chapter offers a focus on the three national champions of the Chinese Internet economy, Baidu, Alibaba, and Tencent

---

[1] Number of outstanding shares multiplied by the share price.

Table 5.2 Profiles of the Chinese BATX (end of 2021)

	Baidu	Alibaba	Tencent	Xiaomi
Founded	2000	1999	1998	2010
Founder	Li Yanhong (Robin Li)	Ma Yun (Jack Ma)	Ma Huateng (Pony Ma) and Zhang Zhidong	Lei Jun
Core business	Search engine	E-commerce	Messaging and gaming	Smartphones
Number of employees	41,000	251,000	86,000	22,000
Key foreign stakeholders	Draper Fisher Jurvetson (USA)	Softbank (Japan), Yahoo (USA)	Naspers (South Africa)	Blackstone (USA)
Headquarter	Beijing	Hangzhou	Shenzhen	Beijing
Patent portfolio	2700	51,500	15,000	34,000
Capitalization	54	374	596	66

Source: published materials

(the case of Xiaomi was analyzed in the previous chapter), and some other smaller actors of the industry. We will see that all the big three succeeded to develop domestically. All three only faced local competitors and few competitors from abroad, either because authorities erected barriers to entry or because foreigners failed to adapt to the Chinese market. All deal with hundreds of millions of customers. As shown by Fig. 5.1, China's first strength is strength in numbers: 1 billion Internet users in 2020—97% of whom use mobile, and also 1.4 billion people using the same writing system (pronunciations vary from one place to another, but writing is unified all over mainland China). The same goes for infrastructure equipment, 4G and new 5G. Baidu, Alibaba, and Tencent developed specific core businesses around which they strongly diversified. All developed strong patent portfolios (for comparison, Microsoft patent portfolio consists of 55,000 grants and 34,000 applications). They were all created by Chinese entrepreneurs in their 30s. All reached impressive market values very quickly—reaching sometimes hundreds of billions of dollars (not millions!).

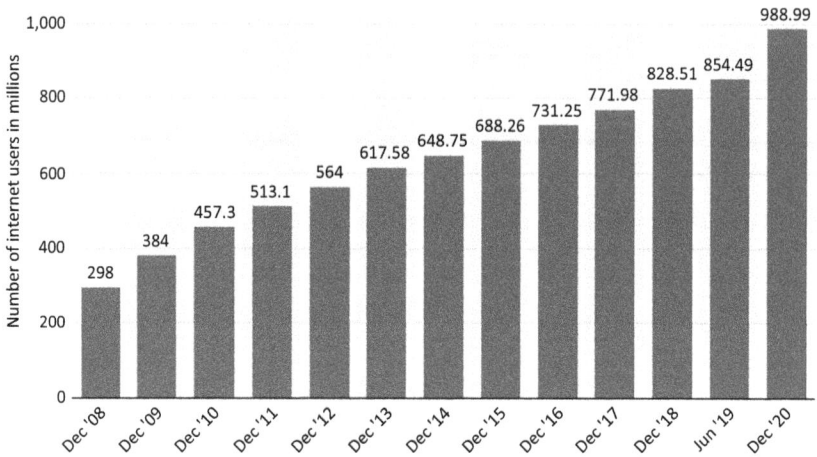

Fig. 5.1 Number of Internet users in China (from 2008 to 2020)

Yet, the big difference between the BATX and the GAFAM is that the BATX are mostly operating in China, whereas the GAFAM are doing a large part of their business outside the USA. Digital China seems to be not soluble with the Western digital sphere.

5.1 Alibaba: The E-commerce Giant

Only 20 Years to Become the World's Largest E-commerce Company

It is a private business created in 1999 (five years after Amazon) in Hangzhou in the wealthy Zhejiang province.[2] Alibaba grew up with the internet in his country. The founder Jack Ma (Ma Yun from his Chinese name) has become a popular personality in China; he owns 7.8% of the group—which makes him one of the biggest fortunes in the country. The

---

[2] The GDP per capita in the Zhejiang province is close to $15,000—higher than the average for China (10,000). Zhejiang is, with Jiangsu, Fujian, Guangdong, amongst the richest provinces in China (all on the coast). The municipalities of Beijing, Shanghai, and Shenzhen are even higher (around $25,000).

epic of the hero of the people fascinates. Jack Ma is a bit the idol of the Chinese as Steve Jobs was the idol of the Americans. The hero started from nothing.

It all began when Jack Ma, working for the Chinese Ministry of Foreign Trade and Economic Cooperation (after having been an English teacher), found himself accompanying Jerry Yang (then boss of Yahoo) on a visit to the Great Wall. It was not long after that Jack Ma launched his B2B site (Alibaba.com), where he offered Chinese companies access to global markets. In 2014, Jack Ma decided at 48 to retire from the position of Managing Director. And in 2018, he made public his succession plan—wishing to step down as President in order to devote himself to education and philanthropy. He effectively handed the reins to Daniel Zhang in 2019 on the occasion of the company's 20th anniversary. While his contemporaries have all, more or less, made copies of foreign models (a Chinese Google, a Chinese Amazon, a Chinese Twitter, etc.), Jack Ma has developed an original model.

It's the Chinese e-commerce giant. Alibaba covers 80% of Chinese e-commerce according to iResearch (Beijing). In fiscal year 2020–2021, its annual revenue bypassed 700 billion yuan, that is, more than $100 billion. The gross merchandising volume generated reached 7.5 trillion yuan for 2020–2021; this is roughly Poland's GDP. The group has grown through a strategy of diversification.

- At the very beginning of the group, with Alibaba.com, it is a marketplace (B2B) that allows Chinese companies to present their products to foreign companies (this Alibaba.com subsidiary was listed in Hong Kong from 2007 to 2012).
- With Taobao.com (literally, the treasure hunt), started in 2003, it is a consumer-to-consumer (C2C) site—like eBay (the US company closed its Chinese branch in 2006). This Taobao site is disputed because it sells many counterfeits (Chanel watches at $78, Louis Vuitton bags at $29, Dior perfumes at $6, etc.). The products are only original in one-third of the cases (according to the State Administration for Industry and Commerce). Alibaba has said it is ready to take action against fakes. But the controversy continues.

- With Tmall.com, started in 2008, it's an online commerce company (B2C)—like Amazon, which claims 500 million users in China. There are 4000 foreign brands that sell their products on Tmall, including some of the best known: Zara, Esprit, Gap, Uniqlo, Cache-cache, or even Mango. Since 2015, Tmall has even offered Japanese products to Chinese consumers.
- With Alipay, launched in 2004, it is an online payment method. This was the Chinese response to PayPal. The number of annual active users of Alipay went from 450 million in 2016 to 900 million in 2019 (according to Statista). Alipay claims over 100 million daily transactions, making mobile payment much more popular than in the USA. Alipay has proven to be perfectly secure. Ant Financial Services Group—the company that runs Alipay—was spun off from Alibaba in 2011. It is no longer just an online payment platform; it has evolved into banking and online wealth management. It even tried at buying American Money Gram in 2018; the move was blocked by CFIUS[3] because it was not feasible for US authorities to give Ant Financial access to sensitive information about US consumers. Ant Financial was valued at $150 billion in 2018; the capitalization bypassed $200 billion in 2020.

Undoubtedly inspired by American Black Friday, Alibaba is, among other things, the promoter in China of Singles Day (numerologically auspicious 11/11) which results each year in an orgy of clicks and a one-off explosion of electronic commerce over just 24 hours (the business went from $25 billion in 2017 to $84 billion in 2021). Alibaba took over an event created in the 1990s by students for singles—who are more and more numerous in China, especially in large cities.

---

[3] The CFIUS is the Committee on Foreign Investment in the USA. Its mission is to reject investment projects in American companies that could affect the security of the nation: defense, critical technologies, technologies affecting infrastructure, and more. For example, it blocked the sale of American semiconductors companies to Chinese companies because the products had military applications. There is even a project of extending the competences of CFIUS to outgoing American investments (toward China).

Ubiquitous Diversification Produced a Comprehensive Ecosystem

Alibaba has built a portfolio of businesses guided by the search for synergies depicted in Fig. 5.2.

E-commerce has become the cash cow for investing in a large number of startups. Alibaba has nearly 1000 subsidiaries, of which more than 400 are outside of China. In 2013, Alibaba acquired Xiami—a music streaming site. Alibaba also took a stake in Weibo (Chinese Twitter), 18% of Youku Tudou (Chinese YouTube) before buying it in its entirety for $4.3 billion, committed $800 million in 2014 to buy 60% of China Vision Media—a Hong Kong-based film and television production company. The company took control of Auto Navi (mapping) for $1.6 billion; the idea is to locate the merchants on its Taobao personal sales site and also to use this application in booking taxis. Alibaba also launched the Tmall Box-Office service inspired by the Netflix model.

Also in 2013, Alibaba launched Yu'e Bao (the "rest of the treasury"), a mutual fund offering better remuneration than deposit banks, that is, 4–6% return compared to the 3% offered by the big banks. Alibaba was emulated by Tencent with Licaitong, then by Xiaomi with Huoqi Bao. Being formally a mutual fund, Yu'e Bao is not subject to the remuneration limits applicable to Chinese banks. Alibaba has raised 600 billion yuan (80 billion euros) in two years! The funds under management passed

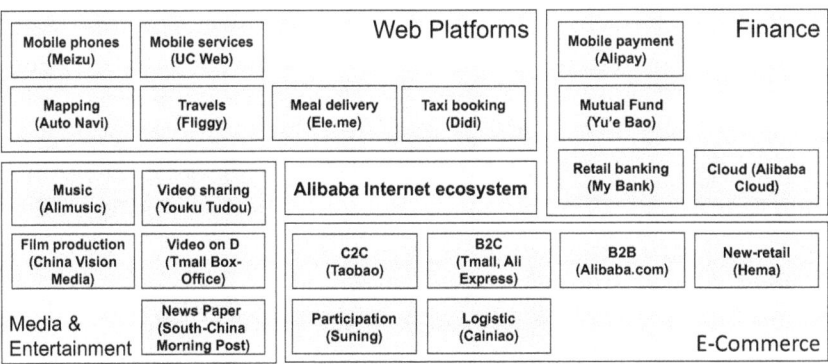

Fig. 5.2 The core business of Alibaba

the 1500 billion yuan (200 billion euros) mark in early 2018. In 2015, after convincing the Chinese government to grant it a license (like five other companies), Alibaba opened MYBank, an online retail bank.

Alibaba is doing everything to switch to electronic commerce through mobile devices (smartphones and tablets); in particular, in 2014, it bought UCWeb (3000 employees), the most popular web browser for smartphones in the country. Alibaba even took a minority stake of $590 million in 2015 in Chinese cellphone maker Meizu. Also in 2015, Alibaba took a stake in Suning, with 1600 stores for four billion euros. And with Ali Cloud, Alibaba has also been in the cloud since 2010. Alibaba is also investing in a global network of R&D in artificial intelligence and announced in 2017 $15 billion of investments over three years. And with Hema stores, Alibaba is blurring the line between virtual stores and brick and cement stores: at Hema, customers scan products, without placing them in their shopping trolleys, and are delivered to their homes. In 2018, Alibaba acquired Ele.me, a readymade products distribution site (valued at $9.5 billion). In short, Alibaba has developed its own ecosystem. Alibaba has become so powerful that the company could afford to take a stake in all the Chinese startups. Such a power could one day be challenged by Chinese authorities or if public opinion believes there is an abuse of dominance.

Foreign Equity Holders

The Japanese technology group Softbank (third mobile telephone operator in Japan, founded by Masayoshi Son, a Japanese billionaire) had contributed $20 million to the creation of Alibaba and it is still in the capital for 34%.

Yahoo had taken 40% of Alibaba in 2005 in exchange for the contribution of its activities in China which the American was struggling to develop—Alibaba was then valued at 2.5 billion dollars. Yahoo has since reduced to 15% (realizing a significant gain in the process). It was precisely the presence of foreigners in his capital that led Jack Ma to pull Ant Financial out of Alibaba—on the grounds that Chinese law did not allow foreigners to own financial businesses.

In September 2014, Alibaba raised $25 billion on the New York Stock Exchange[4] (alongside Walmart and Home-Depot). It was the operation of the year and even a historic turning point. Alibaba surpassed the $22 billion raised by the Agricultural Bank of China in 2010 in Hong Kong and the $16 billion of Facebook in 2012, and it also broke the Visa record in 2008. Alibaba executives initially thought to do this introduction in Hong Kong. But they abandoned the idea because there was no preferential regime in Hong Kong that would have allowed them to keep control of the company, that is, where the founders' shares have more voting rights ("dual-class shares"). The managing authority of the Hong Kong financial center missed the opportunity by refusing to waive. The company is valued at over $400 billion as of 2017—that's the miraculous jackpot for Japanese Softbank and US Yahoo. The value of the Baba share, which had peaked at $119 in November 2014, fell back to less than $60 in September 2015 to return to the $80–100 in the second half of 2016. It has since evolved into the $150–300 range in 2017–2021. Softbank partially realized its capital gain in 2016 by selling $8 billion worth of shares; it still holds the equivalent of $60 billion. After going public in New York in 2014, Alibaba also went public in Hong Kong in 2019.

Expanding Commercially Abroad

The group employed 21,000 people at the end of 2013. At the end of 2014, the workforce reached 34,000 people. The 50,000-employee mark was exceeded in 2017 and went to 251,000 in 2021. Alibaba's activities overall remain 90% concentrated in China. And the boss is targeting the 2 billion customers—enough to turn the company into a "data company." The Chinese market alone still has room for improvement. Ali Express is the structure responsible for the globalization of Alibaba's B2C activities. The group has built up positions in Southeast Asia. But it is eyeing the USA, India, and Russia. The firm launched 11Main in 2014 in the USA—a B2C site comparable to Tmall, but had to resell the site in

---

[4] Since 1999, more than 150 Chinese companies are listed in the USA.

2015 after failing to develop it. Alibaba has also taken a position in India by investing in startups—40% in Paytm (a smartphone payment system) and a stake in Snapdeal, all for $680 million. The group is seeking to use the growing mass of Chinese tourists to convince foreign traders to accept Alipay. In 2016, it launched a global e-commerce platform. Jack Ma is more and more on the political scene, meeting the greats of this world: Australian, Canadian, and Italian prime ministers, among others, and even the President of the USA, Donald Trump. Such an accumulation of power turned into disgrace at the end of 2021 when Chinese government undertook a clampdown on the Chinese tech.

5.2 Baidu: The Search Engine

The Chinese Search Engine

With 74% market share of a market of almost 1 billion Internet users, Baidu is the Goliath which crushes other competitors in China. The second most popular search engine, Sogou, has 19% market share. Baidu arguably responded better than its competitors to the expectations of a younger Internet population with lower incomes and more motivated by entertainment than seeking information. And Baidu didn't have to fight with Google—blocked as early as 2010 by Beijing. Conversely, such a market share creates frustration among users in the absence of a credible alternative and opens the way for public criticism. In fact, the Chinese people are not immune to social media platforms like ByteDance or WeChat. Baidu should pay attention to emerging David's.

Baidu is headquartered in Beijing. The company was established in 2000 by Li Yanhong (Li Robin) with a handful of 20 people. Its workforce increased sharply until 2014, then stabilized around 41,000 employees. Its turnover exceeded 16 billion (dollars) in 2020. Baidu is listed on the Nasdaq (BIDU)—Draper Fisher Jurvetson (DFJ), a US venture capital firm, holds a third of the capital. After reaching peaks in 2018 with a capitalization exceeding $90 billion, it fell back below $50 billion. The company was ranked by the Boston Consulting Group as one of the ten most value-creating companies for the period 2006–2010.

Google Is Not Dead

Baidu does not challenge political orthodoxy; in the eyes of Chinese authorities, the Chinese search engine is much more frequentable than Google. The US company had left the territory of mainland China in 2010 to take refuge in Hong Kong after deciding to no longer apply the rules of self-censorship required by the Chinese political authorities. Google thus finds itself in a marginal position in China—even more so since 2014 when access to Google was prohibited from China. In 2015, however, the press reported on negotiations with the government to return to China with the Google Play app store. Its acquisition of a stake, again in 2015, in the young Chinese artificial intelligence startup Mobvoi (Chumen Wenwen) goes in the same direction. The organization in 2017 of the tournament between its software AlphaGo and the Chinese champion Ke Jie also helps to maintain the link. And in 2018, Google is spending half a billion dollars to take 1% of the capital of the distributor JD.com. There was even talk of coming back with his search engine and meeting Beijing's censorship requirements! And Waymo, Google's autonomous car subsidiary founded in 2009, opened a dedicated subsidiary in China in 2018.

Baidu Diversification Strategy

Baidu is one of the well-established Chinese brands in China. In 2012, Baidu launched its own smartphone, a low-cost model equipped with its Baidu Cloud system (but failed to make it a success). In 2013, Baidu bought "91 Wireless," a subsidiary of NetDragon Websoft specializing in mobile internet, for nearly 1.5 billion euros—a world record for technology in China. The company has been successful in distributing apps (App. Stores) for smartphones over the Internet. Baidu also has its own blogging platform, Baijiahao, and its own video-sharing platform, iQiyi, competitor of Youku Tudou of Alibaba. From 2014 to 2019, Baidu was headed by Zhang Yaqin, the former director of Microsoft's Chinese R&D center (3300 people). Baidu invested $600 million in Uber that same year. In 2015, after Tencent (with WeBank), then Alibaba (with MYBank),

Baidu entered into online retail banking with China Citic Bank (of the state conglomerate Citic Group). The strategy is increasingly based on data collection. Li Yanhong reportedly said, "Baidu knows you better than you know yourself." In fact, Baidu has accumulated an incredible amount of data through the queries made by eight out of ten Chinese on its search engine. If Baidu is a dominant player in China, it is on the other hand—unlike Google—absent from the rest of the world. Baidu makes 2% of its sales outside of China.

Investing in R&D

The percentage of the turnover devoted to R&D has increased from 10% in 2010 to almost 20% today. Baidu is engaged in R&D—particularly in artificial intelligence—with no less than 1300 researchers in this field, and nearly 3000 patents granted. Chinese political leaders believe that artificial intelligence is an area where China has a chance to position itself (see Chap. 7). The company stood out for its capabilities in speech recognition, deep learning, and other big data treatment. Baidu is also betting on smart speakers for home use.

The company is in the self-driving car business with a subsidiary started in 2014 in California under the leadership of a Stanford professor—the idea being to eventually mass-produce these cars. Tests on the Californian public network began in 2016. And real-life tests were conducted in 2017 in China in the Beijing region. Baidu cooperates with Chinese manufacturers such as BYD, Chery, and BAIC and also with foreign OEMs such as Bosch and Continental; on the other hand, the collaboration launched with BMW came to an end. And in 2017, Baidu unveiled Apollo Project—open-source software for autopilot, hoping to make it a dominant design (like Google has done with Android in smartphones); whether this standard potential could extend beyond China's borders remains to be seen. Baidu is also present in auto insurance. In 2021, Baidu presented a concept car of a fully autonomous vehicle. And the company has developed its own AI chip—known as Kunlun.

5.3 Tencent: Gaming and Messaging

A Core Business in Social Media and Gaming

Tencent was founded in 1998 by Pony Ma (51 years old in 2022). It is a private company based in Shenzhen. It employs over 80,000 people. It has experienced an exponential increase in its turnover since its creation: $10 billion in 2013, $15 billion in 2015, $23 billion in 2016, $48 billion in 2018, and $75 billion in 2020. It makes 50% of its turnover with online games. The number of players can be counted in tens, even hundreds of millions. The number of games in the portfolio reaches the thousands—of which only a few are blockbusters. These are games developed in-house but also games purchased from American, South Korean, and even Finnish firms. Tencent took control in 2016 for $8.6 billion of Supercell, the young Finnish startup which created the game *Clash of Clans*. The game *Honor of Kings* is so successful (as mentioned in introduction, with 350 million registered users in China) that Tencent, under Beijing pressure, had to limit the number of hours that young people can play daily. Online gaming activity suffered from the freezing of authorizations to launch new games by the authorities in 2018 (from March to December).

Its second activity is messaging. Tencent launched the online instant messaging service QQ in 1999 and the messaging application for mobile phones Weixin (WeChat in English) in 2011. Many users agree that if WeChat was indeed inspired by an American product, its designers went further. WeChat isn't just for contacting friends. The platform is now used to order meals, to pay bills with Weixin Wallet (WeChat Pay), and even to invest in financial products. The goal is to take all the time the consumer spends online; he must be able to do everything and especially pay for everything with his mobile phone. WeChat exceeded 1 billion monthly active accounts in 2018 worldwide[5] (a user can have multiple active accounts). Advertising is also a growing share of Tencent's revenue. The company carries out the expected checks of the Chinese government; beware, at Tencent, censorship also affects accounts created abroad (among others by the diaspora).

---

[5] Apple Pay has 44 million users in the USA.

A South African Shareholder

Tencent has been listed in Hong Kong since 2004. From 2012 to 2021, the value of Tencent increased by 1400%. In the same period, the Nasdaq increased by 712%. The company's value first ran into billions, then tens of billions, and now hundreds of billions of dollars. At the end of 2017, the $500 billion mark was exceeded. But the capitalization will have lost $200 billion in 2018 after the announcement of poor results (and the temporary ban on launching games). It was back to $500 billion in 2021 (a capitalization lower than Facebook which is around 850). The happiest in Tencent's history are the bosses of South African publisher Naspers, who contributed $34 million to Tencent in 2001 to help the startup grow. The initial investment was certainly diluted from 46.5% to 34% of the capital. But it's valued at over $150 billion, making Naspers the biggest South African company in terms of market value.

Diversification of Functions

Tencent's portfolio is comparable to that of Alibaba: we are witnessing a Chinese remake of the Coca-Pepsi war. It is a question of constantly expanding the range of functions offered: music, portal, search engine, cloud, taxi reservation (in a joint-venture with its competitor Alibaba), and above all, online payment with the Weixin Wallet. Launched on different bases, the two companies Tencent and Alibaba are seeing their portfolios of offers converge. In 2013, Tencent took 36% of Sogou, the country's second largest search engine (subsidiary of Sohu). Tencent is also engaged in the struggle for the domination of online video (streaming); a deal with HBO (Time Warner) gave the Chinese company a legal gateway to American programs (subject to approval by the Censorship Bureau). In 2014, Tencent took 15% of JD.com. In 2017, Tencent Music & Entertainment (TME) and Sweden's Spotify (160 million users) exchanged cross-shareholdings. In 2018, TME was valued at $30 billion. In 2019, Tencent took 10% of Universal Music. Tencent has also embarked on consumer lending business with WeBank—a joint-venture launched after Tencent obtained a retail banking license from the government. Tencent thus serves as a spur to the big public banks. In the automotive industry, Tencent took a 5% stake in Tesla (for $1.78 billion). And Tencent partnered with Guangzhou Automobile Group in 2017 for the development of connected cars.

Tencent tries to internationalize its base, but fails to exceed 100 million users outside of China; the Chinese company will undoubtedly have to go through the acquisition of companies. In the USA, Tencent, in 2017, took $2 billion in the capital of Snap (the parent company of Snapchat). Tencent goes so far as to attack African territory with the support of its first shareholder Naspers (as already mentioned, itself from South Africa). In total, at the end of 2017, Tencent would have invested $4.3 billion in 15 foreign companies (according to Dealogie). Tencent is said to have interests in more than 700 targets. It would have seats on the boards of 400 companies.

Technological Innovation to Prepare the Future

Fifty percent of employees are programmers (software engineers) recruited from college; 25% have a master's degree. The company claims a total of 15,000 patents filed globally on instant messaging, e-business, online payment, search engines, and online games. Tencent was ranked 18th in the "2013 World Most Innovative Companies" by Forbes magazine! And the company is the twelfth of the Top 50 of the "Most Innovative Companies 2015" of the BCG.

5.4 Other Important Players

The picture of the Chinese Internet would be incomplete without the following important actors: Jingdong Mall (JD.com), Yihaodian, and Pinduoduo in the B2C e-commerce, Meituan and Ele.me in food delivery, Didi Chuxing, and ByteDance—the owner of TikTok. Some of these have been able to stay independent; some others were taken over by the big players previously identified.

Jingdong Mall (JD.com), Yihaodian, and Pinduoduo: The Virtual Supermarkets

Jingdong Mall (JD.com), Yihaodian, and Pinduoduo (PDD) are virtual supermarkets. Jingdong made a big splash on the Nasdaq in 2014 and is allied with Tencent. The platform was founded in 1998 in Beijing by Liu Qiangdong (49 years old in 2022), a man from a poor peasant family in Jiangsu. From 300 employees in 2009, the company grew to 120,000 in 2017 (including 65,000 deliverers). The second—Yihaodian—sold 51% of its capital to Walmart. Both have been able to base their development on the strong growth of entry-level smartphones. Pinduoduo was founded in Shanghai in 2016 by Zheng Huang (Colin), a former Google engineer. The company, backed by Tencent, is valued at $33 billion in 2018. It is positioned in low-margin products. The site offers everyday products for which shoppers can decide to make group purchases involving family or friends in order to get discounts. The app is reportedly used by more than 700 million people.

The corollary of virtual supermarkets is the home delivery business, with champions of high-tech logistics like Cainiao (the freight subsidiary from Alibaba). With the explosion of e-commerce came also the emergence of a fragmented logistics industry with its army of home delivery men on scooters or electric tricycles who don't count their hours. It is the low cost of these couriers that allows customers to have a simple box of Kleenex delivered to them. These "disposable" couriers are the slaves of modern times: such as low pay, extended working hours, and poor social protection. New rules were issued in 2021 to improve their working conditions.

With its own fleet of cargo planes, SF Express stands out; its boss, Wang Wei, succeeded in federating a group of regional logistics companies. In this battle for logistics, I also have to name firms like Best Logistics and Global Logistic Properties (GLP).

Meituan and Ele.me: The Chinese Uber Eats

In this food delivery industry, Ele.me and Meituan form now a duopoly. Ele.me (Alibaba) and Meituan (Tencent) are in a knife fight. This is an

$80 Billion market in China. This activity is incidentally an environmental disaster with its plastic cutlery and containers.

Ele.me was created in 2008 by Zhang Xuhao and Kang Jia in Shanghai. It's a platform which organizes the home distribution of readymade products. It connects restaurants and eaters. Step by step, it succeeded in covering more than 2000 cities in China. It was acquired in 2018 by Alibaba (valued at $9.5 billion). The same year, Ele.me merged with the Baidu Takeaway business (Waimai)—which Baidu failed to develop.

Meituan started in 2010 as a Chinese equivalent of Groupon. Based in Beijing, the company was founded by Wang Xing (43 years old in 2022). At the end of 2015, Meituan and Dianping (a restaurant review site linked to Tencent) concluded a merger. Less than a year later, Meituan–Dianping is valued at over $18 billion, and more than $200 billion since 2020. Meituan–Dianping is the largest home- or office-meal delivery company in the world. The business is organized on the same model as Uber Eats; it works with restaurants (6 million) and couriers and liaises with customers (600 million). Meituan raised $4.2 billion in Hong Kong in 2018. Its first two shareholders are Tencent and Sequoia Capital. It was valued in 2018 at $50 billion. It now offers more than 200 online services which account for 40% of its turnover.

Didi: Better Fitted to Its Territory Than Uber

In February 2015, the two Chinese internet giants Tencent and Alibaba agreed to merge their respective smartphone booking applications for taxis or passenger cars with driver. Didi Dache (literally "beep-beep calls a taxi") and Kuaidi Dache (literally "quick taxi") come together to form the Goliath Didi Kuaidi. Together they represent 100% of the taxi market and 80% of the private driver market (note that private taxis remained technically illegal in China until 2016 when the government legalized the activity). The merger aims to counter Uber in China.

Entered in Shanghai in August 2013, the Californian gradually expanded through major cities. Faced with a competitor so well aligned with his territory, Uber's battle against Didi was bitter. Each competitor fought with its rebates to passengers to build up a base. Uber's trump card was its deal with Baidu in December 2014 to help it penetrate the field. It was doing 100,000 daily rides in June 2015. Uber was at daggers drawn with Didi Kuaidi. By mid-2016, it claimed to have 150 million monthly users; it would have captured 10% of the market. Also in 2016, it was Apple that invested $1 billion in Didi Chuxing—the new name of Didi Kuaidi, no doubt to be seen in Beijing (and also to invest in the automotive field). China Merchants Bank is also committing $2.5 billion.

Twist in July 2016: Uber transfers its Chinese activities to Didi Chuxing and ends up with 20% of the Chinese capital (12.8 in 2021). This is the end of the competition between the two giants. The Uber–Baidu alliance will not have been enough. Didi is valued at $56 billion in early 2019. But would be much less profitable than Uber on the run (3% vs. 20%). Passenger murders committed in 2018 by drivers cast doubt on Didi's control over its drivers. In 2021, Didi had 377 million users and 13 million drivers.

Since 2017, Didi is no longer satisfied with the sole Chinese territory, where it still has to face 200 competitors (admittedly much smaller) and where a possible diversification in the distribution of meals is unlikely in view of the two big players already in place in this activity (Ele.me and Meituan). The Chinese company was tackling Uber to take positions outside China. Didi has taken a series of stakes in the largest markets: the USA, India, Southeast Asia, the Middle East, and even Eastern Europe. Didi also bought "99" in Brazil.

Didi even aims to launch its own autonomous car (to no longer have to pay drivers); it rallied a whole group of automotive companies and made the business a subsidiary (as Uber also did). The aim is to make better use of its base of 450 million active users of its services. Didi launched its robotic taxi service (without driver) in Shanghai in 2019 in the Jiading district (SAIC and BMW have also received licenses), while Uber abandoned the business of driverless cars in 2020. The company went public in New York in 2021 and raised $4.4 billion there (Alibaba, when it joined New York in 2014, had raised $25 billion). Shortly after the IPO, the Chinese Cyberspace Administration questioned Didi's handling of personal information and ordered its removal from app stores in China.

ByteDance

The company ByteDance was created in 2011 by Zhang Yiming (40 years old in 2022). One of its businesses is the Chinese equivalent of Yahoo News: Jinri Toutiao aggregates news content using artificial intelligence while playing the card of personalization. Users number in the tens of millions. Created in 2012, it is valued at more than $10 billion in 2017. In 2018, however, it was called to order by the authorities to show more respect for socialist values.

ByteDance launched Douyin in 2016, which became TikTok outside of China, an application that allows to share short videos (15 seconds). It claimed 300 million monthly users in 2018; 700 million was reached in July 2020. ByteDance was valued at $75 billion in 2019. The platform is said to have developed in more than 150 countries—notably after the acquisition of Musical.ly in 2017. With 200 million users, India is its second market after China. It would censor content related to the Chinese government beyond China's borders. Contested in the USA, TikTok came close to banishment. As a result, the company chose to transfer data on US users from China to the USA and Singapore. TikTok also opened a "transparency and accountability center" in the USA and an identical center in Europe.

Unsurprisingly, ByteDance has branched out into e-commerce, music streaming, and mobile video game publishing. The platform has doubled its revenue in 2020 to reach $34 billion. In 2021, ByteDance started selling artificial intelligence technology applications to Internet companies in China and outside of China—competing with companies like Amazon Web Services, Google, or IBM. An IPO is planned.

5.5 Conclusion

While catching up was the target of the Chinese government, overtaking foreign companies in mature industries was unthinkable. As an emerging industry, the Internet was the playground where Chinese companies started without a strong handicap, more or less on an equal footing with others. Besides this specific status, all the companies examined in this chapter have common features regarding their strategy. They are all:

- Strongly connected with the Chinese authorities. That's a key point in China, without connections with the authorities (the State and the Communist Party), you do nothing.
- Private companies which got a mandate given by the Chinese authorities. To foster the development of local champions, the State instituted some forms of protectionism, precluding US and other foreign companies from penetrating the Chinese market and, at the same time, protecting its cyber sovereignty.
- Backed up by Chinese, but also foreign, investment companies.
- Exhibiting a good match with the local demand. Chinese people use the same writing system, but they are far from being uniform. Chinese companies are in a better position to understand their market particularities than foreign companies.
- Used to external growth to implement their diversification strategies and have fostered development through acquisition of successful startups.
- Have based their development on diversification strategies after consolidating their initial core business.
- Significantly diversified on the Internet. They started with different businesses, but because of successive diversifications, they tend toward comparable portfolios—as illustrated by Table 5.3.
- Centered on their business in China, and weakly present outside China. They might already be satisfied with the huge Chinese market. Another explanation is that rules are quite different outside China, and the GAFAM (and others) already have taken positions.
- Preparing the future with major technology investments, investing strongly in R&D, using other means such as startup takeover to gain access to innovation, and building serious patent portfolios.
- Have, over the years, accumulated impressive data on the behaviors of their (Chinese) customers; and this is what they are going to sell in the future.

Table 5.3 Comparing BATX business portfolios

	Baidu	Alibaba	Tencent	Xiaomi
B2B C2C B2C Hybrid Distribution brick and mortar		Alibaba.com Taobao Tmall Hema Suning	JD.com (17.1%)	
Food delivery		Ele.me	Meituan (17.2%)	
Payment	Du Xiaoman	Alipay	WeChat pay	Mi Pay
Online retail banking	Du Xiaoman	My Bank	WeBank (30%)	Xin Wang Bank (29.5%)
Mutual fund	Du Xiaoman Licai	Yu'e Bao	Licaitong	Huo Qi Bao
Honk Kong virtual banking license		Ant SME Services (Hong Kong)	Fusion Bank (joint-venture)	Insight Fintech HK Limited (90%)
Search engine	Baidu.com	Quark	Sogou (36%)	
Mapping	Baidu Map	Auto Navi	Tencent Maps	
Cloud	Baidu Cloud	Ali Cloud		
Blogging	Baijiahao			
Music streaming	Baidu Music	Xiami	Tencent Music & Entertainment	Mi Music
Video streaming	iQiyi	Youku Tudou	Tengxun Shipin	
Production		China Vision Media	Universal Music (10%)	
Equivalent of Netflix		Tmall BoxOffice		

This chapter shows that while the strategy of international Chinese companies turned out to be a good fit for national development, it might not work for international expansion. In a business which is more and more data driven, BAT collected limited data on non-Chinese consumers. Yet, the companies which are more focused, like Didi or ByteDance, are more internationalized. They might prefigure the future of Chinese companies.

China has also opened a door to exportation of all those new technologies through the Belt and Road Initiative (BRI); the new silk road is not only on earth and on the sea, this is also a digital road fostering connectivity. Telecommunications networks, internet connections, the BeiDou satellite navigation system (the Chinese GPS), cloud computing, fiber-optic cables, IOT, railways digital infrastructures, logistic automation, enterprise resources planning are applications desired by all countries on the new silk roads. There are also plans to establish science parks in several of those countries.

References

Jolly, D. (2021). Is China going to run the digital world? In F. Spigarelli & J. R. McIntyre (Eds.), *The new Chinese dream: Industrial transition in the post-pandemic era* (pp. 69–85). Palgrave Macmillan. isbn:978-3-030-69811-9.

Kim, Y.-C., & Chen, P.-C. (2018). *The digitization of business in China*. Palgrave Macmillan Asian Business Series.

McKinsey Global Institute. (2017, August). *China's digital economy*. A leading global force, Discussion paper.

6

Applications in Other Industries: From Technological Catch-up to International Development

Abstract This chapter looks at others industries where China succeeded to catch up beyond telecommunications and the Internet. Despite contrasted morphological profiles, the four industries examined exhibit several commonalities. Again, learning from foreign competitors, scale effects achieved in China, and the strong control of the authorities are key. In addition, a general rule is that Chinese companies started to build positions in their home country before tackling international markets; the status of national champions gained thanks to the massive Chinese market that helped Chinese firms to establish their legitimacy outside of China. Progressiveness also occurred with the depth of the involvement in the value-chain: when Chinese firms enter one industry, they first rely on foreign suppliers for sophisticated parts before trying in a second phase to emancipate. For example, the Chinese high-speed train still relies on foreign suppliers for some specific parts. The challenge for Chinese firms is to internalize the design and the production of those parts.

Keywords Catch-up • Internationalization • Manufacturing • Value-chain • Robotization

In addition to the telecommunications and the Internet, Chinese companies have invested in several other high-tech sectors. Four industries are considered here: rare earth, photovoltaic panels, high-speed train, and nuclear plants—where catch-up occurred (Keun et al. 2017). As shown in Table 6.1, the reasons for choosing those industries are because they cover different stages of different value chains, serve different types of customers, and exhibit different levels of technological intensity.

The last section of this chapter is devoted to manufacturing. Within most of the industries reviewed in this chapter, several Chinese companies succeeded in catching up technologically with the West. After developing commercially in China, they are now positioned on international markets (Alon & McIntyre, 2007). In those industries, the success of Chinese companies is not due to their inventiveness, but to their ability to learn from the West and reproduce in China innovations originated from the USA or Europe. To reaffirm their success, they need to go to the next step. Here is the challenge for China: being able to go further than simply reproducing, but developing truly innovative solutions; that's the issue of indigenous innovation as stressed in Chap. 2. As usual, in China, all those industries developed thanks to a massive demand and the efficient exploitation of scale effects (Yeung et al., 2011). This chapter is based on a review of published materials on those sectors over the last ten years; it uses a cross-section perspective.

Table 6.1 Overview of the industries analyzed in Chap. 6

Industry	Nature of the business	Technological intensity	China's advantage	Scale effect
Rare earth	Supply of raw materials (B2B)	Materials sold to high-tech industries	Lower ecological constraints	Worldwide quasi-monopoly
Photovoltaic panels	Manufacturing of finished products (B2C)	R&D is spent on cells	Scale and low production costs	Largest manufacturer in the world
High-speed train	Business to government (B2G)	High	Digestion of Western technologies	Largest high-speed train network
Nuclear plants	Business to government (B2G)	High	Collaboration with foreign companies	Fast follower of the USA, France, and Japan

6.1 Rare Earth: A Chinese Worldwide Quasi-Monopoly

China Became a Leader After the USA Stopped Their Own Production

Cerium, dysprosium, or neodymium oxide are metals with specific physical properties, either magnetically or optically. The extraction of rare earth is not a high-tech industry. Their extraction is highly polluting and it consumes energy. Yet, those materials are used in the manufacture of many technological products such as batteries, catalysts for catalytic converters, hard disks, mobile phones, permanent magnets for wind turbines, LEDs, and military equipment such as missile guidance systems. The use may be limited: there are 2.2 pounds of neodymium in the batteries of a Toyota Prius. But the needs can also be much greater: 400 kilos of neodymium are needed to make a wind turbine. Japan is the world's largest consumer of rare earths—ahead of the USA.

Contrary to what one might think, rare earths are abundant on earth—but scattered. China, Brazil, Vietnam, Russia, India, and Australia have the largest reserves. China holds a third of the world's known geological reserves. Since the USA virtually stopped extracting rare earths in the late 1990s, China concentrates 95% of world production (130,000 tons per year). The Baotou deposit (Inner Mongolia) holds an important place. China also has reserves in Jiangxi with the company JL Mag Rare-Earth based in Ganzhou (Jiangxi). With such a quasi-monopoly, China depends on foreign countries to sell its production as alternatives exist, but can also exert pressure. This domination of production creates tensions in the market. China implemented a quota policy in the 2000s. This resulted in a sharp rise in prices.

Looking for Solutions

Foreign companies then embarked on alternative routes to face quotas: relaunching the exploitation of mines (old or new), developing a recycling sector, and researching alternative technologies that do not use rare earths. The rise in prices of these raw materials thus led the American firm Molycorp, producer of rare earths in the USA, to restart in 2012 production at the Mountain Pass mine (on the border between California and Nevada)—the mine had been discovered in 1949, stopped in 2002, sold in 2008 by Chevron to Molycorp. But it filed for bankruptcy in 2015. The mine was sold in 2017 to MP (Mountain Pass) Mine Operations. The operation was relaunched in 2021 with the objective of ensuring 16% of world production. Australia has a plan to open a mine by Lynas (at Mount Weld, a site reputed to be the third in the world after Baotou and Mountain Pass) that could be of interest to Japan.

To escape the quotas, Japanese firms have relocated near Baotou. The Chinese quotas were finally lifted in 2015 under pressure from the WTO following action by Japan, the USA, and Europe. But in 2019, after the USA raised tariffs on Chinese imports, President Xi Jinping reignited the debate by reminding China's key role in rare earth world supplies. This is arguably what prompted President Joe Biden to push for reopening Mountain Pass.

6.2 The Photovoltaic Business: China Overtook the USA and Europe

The photovoltaic industry is one of the components of the green strategy of the Chinese government for sustainability and de-carbonization. It comes with other industries like windmills, bioenergy, nuclear (see next section), new energy vehicles (see next chapter), and smart grids.

The photoelectric effect was discovered at the end of the nineteenth century. But, the business really took off during the 1960s in the USA and in Europe with niche markets such as the space and electricity supply in outlying areas. The USA and Europe lost the battle on photovoltaic panels. From producing less than 1% of solar panels in 2000, China now supplies 70% of photovoltaic panels globally. Europeans, but also Americans, have regularly complained about China's anti-competitive behavior. This has been the case for Chinese photovoltaic panels on which the Europeans had imposed taxes while the bankruptcies of manufacturers of photovoltaic panels had multiplied in Europe (Solon, Q-Cells, Conergy, Photowatt), as in the USA (Solyndra, Evergreen Solar). The fight was embodied from 2010 to 2014 by Karel De Gucht, European Commissioner for Trade, who brought several accusations against China. An agreement on a floor price and a sales ceiling was finally reached in 2013 on solar panels.

6 Applications in Other Industries: From Technological... 101

China has been the leading investor in renewable energies since 2013 (followed by the USA, Japan, Germany, and India); in 2014, the country installed ten gigawatts of photovoltaic panels, notably in the west of the country (as in Dunhuang in Gansu province). China now has the lion's share of the global total for wind turbines and photovoltaic installations. The pace of equipment has undoubtedly decreased as the government reduced its subsidies in 2018.

The industry is not only a set of successes. China has also experienced setbacks in photovoltaics. The most emblematic case is the bankruptcy of Suntech. It's a remarkable illustration of the danger of investing in production capabilities when one industry flirts with overcapacity.

Vignette: Suntech

The company Suntech was founded in 2001 by Shi Zhengrong after his studies in Australia. He responded to a request from the authorities in Wuxi (west of Shanghai) where he was originally from. Suntech experiences a meteoric rise in just a few years and became the largest Chinese manufacturer of photovoltaic cells. The company is driven by low labor costs and central government incentives for renewable energies (since they can reduce the weight of coal and oil). It is notably supported by the China Development Bank. In 2005, the group is listed on the New York Stock Exchange. In 2006, the founder becomes the biggest Chinese fortune. In 2007, the group employs 4000 people. In 2010, the company opens a factory in Arizona. In 2011, Suntech is consecrated as world number one in photovoltaic cells. It employs 17,700 persons. Its market value was $16 billion. But innovation remains limited: the company mainly buys production equipment abroad (in the USA, Germany, Switzerland, and Japan) and develops large-scale production in China to reduce costs.

After a decade of strong growth and massive investment, the industry entered a phase where supply exceeded demand. In 2012, there was a demand equivalent to 35 GW for an installed production capacity of 50 GW. Suntech had a loss of $1 billion for fiscal 2011. The company urgently obtained bank financing under pressure from the local government in Wuxi. In early 2013, Suntech was unable to repay a series of matured bonds. The Chinese company must file for bankruptcy. It went bankrupt with $1.4 billion in debt. Doctor Shi is gradually disembarked. The stock is set at one dollar on the New York Stock Exchange. The effect on suppliers is direct; for example, a company like L'Air Liquide suffered from the bankruptcy of Suntech. The central government is no longer ready to support any business at any cost. After Suntech's bankruptcy, its production assets were taken over by Shunfeng (from Changzhou, Jiangsu)—thus not reducing the sector's overcapacity.

Its competitor, Yingli Solar—which was amongst the stars of the field for a time—was taken off the New York Stock Exchange in 2018, where it had been admitted in 2007. Like Suntech, Yingli has had to suffer from overcapacity of the sector.

6.3 The Chinese High-Speed Train: Technological Digestion

An Example of Technological Digestion

The Chinese high-speed train is one of the most tangible illustrations of the Chinese concept known as "technological digestion": the local teams fed themselves with the various high-speed train programs in the world, digested all these inputs, and produced their own train. This product, designed by Chinese engineers, owes a great deal to the many collaborations carried out over the years with the main global players in railway equipment. At the heart of these contracts is the deal with Kawasaki Heavy Industries—which is the Japanese company behind the Shinkansen. Chinese high-speed train companies had also collaborations with Siemens—the manufacturer of the ICE—the German high-speed train, Alstom—the manufacturer of the French TGV—and Bombardier. Chinese high-speed train still relies today on several components (such as transmission, brakes, or control software) supplied by foreign companies such as Alstom, Siemens, and Kawasaki Heavy Industries.

Thousands of Kilometers

The program started very recently: before 2007, there was no high-speed train in China. However, since 2017, China has the largest high-speed train network in the world (with 22,000 km of lines). After having crisscrossed the east of the country, it attacked the center and the west (as far as Xinjiang). Twenty-five thousand kilometers were reached in 2018, 35,000 kilometers in 2020. A doubling of the network is in perspective for 2035. Rail is an illustration of the potential size effects of China. This size allows the Chinese to have significant R&D teams on subjects such as, for example, permanent magnet synchronous transmission (which makes it possible to reduce consumption and noise in particular). However, this development was accompanied by massive indebtedness of China Railway.

International Markets as the Target

The Chinese high-speed train program experienced a dramatic episode with the Wenzhou accident in July 2011. If this fatal crash undermined the international ambitions of the program's leaders, China still managed to sell its high-speed train to many countries. That's the case in Laos for the 1000 kilometers link between Kunming (Yunnan) and Vientiane (in exchange for deliveries of potash and copper ore); the connection started to operate in October 2021. A project in Turkey has been completed between Ankara and Istanbul. A contract was also signed with Indonesia in 2015 for the Jakarta-Bandung line. China started also the construction of a high-speed line in Thailand (a north-south project linking Kunming to Singapore). The Chinese high-speed train could one day find an outlet in links between major African capitals. Projects exist as well in Argentina, Mexico, and even the USA on the project between Las Vegas and Los Angeles. This 370-kilometer project, which was to be entrusted to China Railway International, was however denounced in 2016 under the pressure of the US authorities. If the Chinese companies can win bids on rolling stock, it will be more difficult for them to impose themselves on infrastructure in the USA, where they cannot employ Chinese workers. Likewise, projects in Venezuela, Libya, Mexico, and Myanmar have been abandoned.

By order of the State Council, the two Chinese entities that produce high-speed train—CNR (China Northern Rolling Stock) and CSR (China Southern Rolling Stock)—were merged in 2015 to make a single entity capable of positioning itself in the global plan. The government wants to prevent destructive competition. It didn't want to see its champions fall into the trap of price wars overseas. The new China Railway Rolling Stock Corporation (CRRC) represents a company of 170,000 employees, with a turnover of more than $30 billion. It is building on American soil (Springfield, Massachusetts) a car manufacturing unit for the Boston subway. It undoubtedly welcomed with great relief the announcement of the European Community, which adopted an exactly opposite posture with the ban on the merger between Alstom and Siemens.

6.4 The Nuclear Plants: A Fast Development

The First Worldwide Market

In 1980, China was a dwarf in the civilian nuclear industry. It has since become the world's leading market for the construction of power plants. This ambitious program was barely slowed down by the Fukushima disaster. China is experiencing a rise in power: there are 20 power plants in operation and 28 under construction (vs. 100 in operation in the USA and 10 under construction, and, respectively, 58 and 2 in France, and 48 and 12 in Japan). In this area, the role of the state is hegemonic. Energy supply is unambiguously a national challenge, as China became since 2009 the largest consumer of energy on the planet ahead of the USA. It cannot develop without nuclear energy if it wants to reduce its dependence on coal and its corollary CO_2 emissions. The uranium needs are met by national production and purchases on the world market.

Borrowing from Developed Countries

Nuclear is one of those fields where the Chinese authorities have turned to foreigners to learn the business. There are two state-owned Chinese companies which are building nuclear power plants. Each is allied with a leading foreign manufacturer; China is used to this strategy of multiplying the access channels. The point was already mentioned in Chap. 2 with alliances portfolio (cf. the example of FAW) or in the previous section about the high-speed train. Thus, China General Nuclear Power Group (CGNPG)—based in Shenzhen—partnered with the French Areva and EDF and China National Nuclear Corporation (CNNC)—based in

Beijing—set up an alliance with Westinghouse–Toshiba. Westinghouse transferred the AP1000 technology to the Chinese nuclear industry in 2006. The Taishan 1 plant (in Guangdong) is one of the five plants around the world based on European Power Reactor (EPR) technology. Taishan Nuclear Power Joint Venture Company (TNPJVC) is 51% owned by the Chinese utility China General Nuclear Power Corporation (CGN), 30% by EDF, and 19% by the Chinese utility Guangdong Energy Group. Chinese power thus allows China to access the world's best knowledge in this area. The Chinese companies have been the builders of their own power plants for many years. The Hualong 1 (or ACP 1000), a third generation reactor (of 1000 megawatts), was certified in 2014. The Chinese are clearly announcing their desire to become independent.

On the Way for International Markets

The construction of reactors is not limited to China. The Chinese authorities are looking to sell power plants around the world. The two Chinese companies have thus won contracts in Pakistan (for the construction of six reactors) and in the UK in the south-west of England at Hinkley-Point (EDF brings the technology and CGNPG part of the financing) for a total cost of 33 billion euros. There have, however, been protests in the UK from people concerned about security issues and threats to national security. Because of their change of government in 2016, the project was delayed by the British new administration. In Argentina, two plants will be built by China National Nuclear Corporation (CNNC), one using Canadian technology and the other 100% Chinese. China is also providing funding for the $15 billion project. From then on, China joined the very closed club of nuclear power plant exporting countries (the USA, Japan, France, Russia, South Korea, and Canada). The Chinese are even expected to supply components to power plants currently under construction in the USA (Georgia and North Carolina). China finds itself with the power to redesign the geography of the electrical industry, technologies, OEMs, and more. A Chinese entry into Areva's capital is also under consideration. The processing of nuclear fuels is also the subject of Sino-French cooperation.

In 2021, China announced a program to build 150 new nuclear power plants in China on the base of their Hualong technology, and 30 outside China on the new silk road. This will reduce demand for coal and reduce CO_2 emissions. This is also going to be a challenge for countries like the USA and France.

6.5 Manufacturing Industries

Made in China 2025 Plan

Despite the sharp rise in costs and the loss of the associated competitive advantage, the Chinese government is not abandoning the manufacturing field, as evidenced by the national plan published in 2015 entitled "Made in China 2025." China wants to remain a manufacturing powerhouse. Yet, the future of the Chinese economy cannot be to continue manufacturing underwear for the whole planet. The plan launched in 2015 by Premier Li Keqiang aims to improve the performance of the manufacturing industry, to move China from a labor-intensive manufacturing economy to more high-tech and, above all, more efficient industrial and service activities. This is to avoid falling into the trap of middle-income economies by modernizing the industry by infusing it with more advanced technologies (see Chap. 8). It identified ten priority areas: advanced information technologies (such as artificial intelligence and quantum communication), robots, space and aeronautics, shipyards, rail, self-driving cars and vehicles, new automotive engines, energy production, agricultural equipment, new materials, and bio-pharmacy.

Priority is given to innovation, increased productivity, restructuring, upscaling, and internationalization. China wants to free itself from its dependence on foreign companies. Foreigners saw the "Made in China 2025" plan as a way to force foreign firms to disclose their technologies in exchange for access to the Chinese market. This is why authorities in 2018 asked Chinese media not to refer to the term. The aim is to encourage the emergence of national champions in ten industries with high technological content—such as cars using alternative propulsion to the gasoline engine. Could this be the comeback of the well-known Maoist slogan "Rely on our own strength"? The traditional suppliers of machine tools—Germany and Switzerland, in particular—should still find some benefits.

Increasing Automation

One of the challenges facing China is the extreme diversity of its manufacturing tool in its economy: there are companies with modern manufacturing resources—like Sany (construction machinery) or Goldwind (wind turbines)—but also companies with particularly rustic means. The "Made in China 2025" plan therefore aims to develop a sophisticated and efficient manufacturing base. Investing in automation is seen as the only way to keep China's industrial base competitive.

Sales of robots have grown strongly around the world since 2010 (at a rate of +19% per year between 2012 and 2017). Annual installations of industrial robots stabilized around 400,000 per year since 2017. They were mainly driven by Asia and in particular by China. The Chinese industries have come a long way: in China, there were only 11 robots installed for 10,000 employees in 1997 versus a ratio numbering in the tens or even hundreds in the most advanced industrial nations at that time. Since 2013, China became the world's largest buyer. As shown by Fig. 6.1, robot density went to 246 robots per 10,000 employees in 2020 (it was at 187 in 2019 and only 97 in 2017). China now surpassed the global average of 126 robots per 10,000 employees.

The ratio remains much higher in leading countries: 932 in South Korea, 605 in Singapore, 390 in Japan, and 371 in Germany (source: International Federation of Robotics). But, in the end, China now has the largest fleet of robots in the world in absolute terms.

Foreign robot manufacturers like Fanuc, Yaskawa, Kawasaki, Nabtesco, ABB, Omron, Stäubli, and others such as Kuka can't wait when they see the emergence of alternatives to the automotive market. Kuka had been the target of a takeover bid by the Chinese Midea in 2016 for 4.5 billion

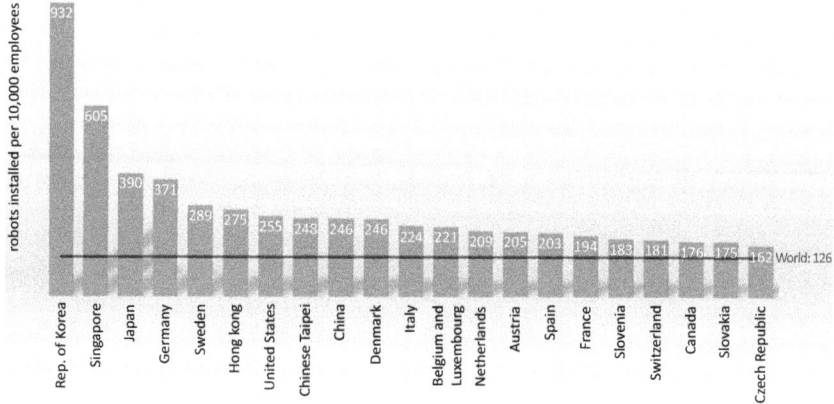

Fig. 6.1 Robot density in the manufacturing industry 2020

euros. This takeover of Kuka is at the heart of the "Made in China 2025" plan. Chinese robot makers (like Siasun, Estun, Huashu, or Kejie) are emerging—largely supported by the Chinese government. While Chinese companies are taking a growing share of the robot market, the key parts of these robots (controllers, speed reducers, and servo motors) are often still produced by foreign companies. In addition, a good part of the robots installed in China were bought by foreign firms.

Still, most analysts agree that manufacturing's share of GDP should decline to make room for more services. In fact, the weight of these in the GDP has not stopped increasing for 20 years. The 50% milestone was reached in 2015 (compared to figures between 60% and 80% in developed economies). Services should develop and also gain in productivity in areas such as education, health, the senior market, insurance, financial services, and logistics.

6.6 Conclusion

This chapter examined four industries. All are different in terms of customers, technological intensity, and the stage of the value-chain covered. Despite this variety, those examples show how Chinese companies have been able to learn from worldwide foreign leaders. Technological catch-up is a condition to target international markets. Different means were used including licensing agreements, acquisition of equipment, joint-ventures, consortiums, and so on. Different wordings were used: borrowing, reproduction, digestion, and catch-up, among others. But the Chinese strategy has always been the same: to gain access to the best knowledge in the world.

If learning from developed countries has been the common thread to all cases, each case has its own specificities. Rare earth extraction took a quasi-monopoly competitive position because China accepted levels of pollution we would not accept. The photovoltaic panel industry has been able to challenge European and US firms which originally started this business, but failed to develop it. Chinese companies had exploited their cost advantage with labor. But, they have also been able to go farther.

The process is never all at once. It is always progressive, done step by step. Establishing solid bases in China comes before tackling international markets. And, dependence on external suppliers is frequently accepted in a first stage. But, the aim of emancipation is always targeted as a second step.

Another common thread is the key role played by Chinese authorities. The point is obvious for BTG activities: Beijing forced companies to merge in the high-speed train, and Beijing promoted nuclear plants along the new silk roads. But this chapter also shows the intervention of Chinese authorities in the rare earth and photovoltaic businesses.

A final recurring characteristic is the efficient exploitation of scale effects. The Chinese companies perform well in taking advantage of a massive market. And, this also serves their interest when they internationalize.

Yet, the question still remains: many Chinese companies have been able to reproduce—frequently on a larger scale—what has been invented abroad. Will those Chinese companies be able to go further, that is, to be proactive actors in the future generations of technologies and products? This is the subject of Chap. 7.

References

Alon, I., & McIntyre, J. R. (2007). *Globalization of Chinese enterprises* (p. 272). Palgrave Macmillan.

Keun, L., Gao, X., & Li, X. (2017). Industrial catch-up in China: A sectoral systems of innovation perspective. *Cambridge Journal of Regions, Economy and Society, 10*(1), 59–76.

Yeung, A., Poertsch, W., Liu, S., & Kathrin, X. (2011). *The globalization of Chinese companies: Strategies for conquering international markets* (p. 224). Wiley.

7

Applications of the Future

Abstract Two different situations are examined. On one hand, there is the space industry where China has been involved for decades, with two big entities under state control, and which is still promising. On the other hand, there are emerging businesses which are new for China but also new for the world: the car of the future, the block-chain, the artificial intelligence, and the Fintech. They exhibit the traditional features of emerging high-tech businesses: academia is the source of knowledge, born global, plenty of startups are emerging, competition is fragmented, the ecosystem has to be put in place, and rules of the game need to be written. The Chinese authorities have a clear mindset about the future technological trajectory of those domains: they are the conductor; they show the way. But political leaders fully entrusted to the performers, that is, to the market, the upcoming of those industries.

Keywords Emerging sectors • Market forces • Fragmented industries • Born global • Knowledge-driven • Top-down

To gain global leadership, Chinese authorities developed clear plans to achieve competitive advantages in several industries. Among the applications prioritized by the Chinese authorities, the chapter will focus on five different sectors:

- The space
- The electric-powered and driverless cars
- The block-chain
- The artificial intelligence
- The Fintech

For the last four examples, the core argument is not to try to compete in mature industries where advanced nations have an advantage. In the car industry, for example, Chinese car manufacturers cannot compete with German car manufacturers who have been in this ecosystem for more than a century. There are very limited perspectives for the combustion engine—because of ecological concerns—but also because no technological breakthrough can be envisioned, and only incremental innovation can be expected. On the opposite, Chinese companies can compete with alternative propulsion engines as competitors from advanced nations have just recently entered this domain. And, as usual, emerging industries frequently come with a high number of new entrants. This competition favors the emergence of solid models elected by the market.

7.1 An Established Space Industry

China Has Accumulated a Long Experience of Space Missions

The examples further analyzed in this chapter were all developed recently (less than two decades). Space is different from those examples; it has long been a high-tech island in a low-tech ocean. The Chinese space program started in 1956, in association with the Soviets. Authorities recognized a military vocation to this program, that is, the development of combat capabilities in space—including for offensive and coercive purposes. The first Chinese satellite was launched in 1970. The first man was sent into the space (and came back alive) in October 2003, along with Shenzhou V. Since then, taikonaut flights have followed one another. In 2013, the Chinese "Jade Rabbit" rover (inspired by its American counterpart Curiosity) made its first moonwalk after being dropped there by a Long-March rocket. New missions followed. In 2017, China launched its first cargo rocket. At the end of 2018, China, for the first time in history, managed to land the Chang'e 4 probe on the face of the moon not visible from the earth—a challenge to the Americans. And the Chinese have managed to germinate (briefly) cotton seeds in a confined atmosphere.

A Chinese Space Station Has Been Initiated

A new future Chinese Space Station called Tiangong (Celestial Palace) was built in Tianjin (half an hour by high-speed train from Beijing), and the project was initially launched in 1992. A first module, the so-called central part Tianhe-1 (Celestial Harmony), was launched by a Long March rocket in April 2021 from Hainan. Two other elements, Wentian and Mengtian, are to follow. This space station should be operational in 2022; it is planned to operate in low earth orbit (between 340 and 450 km altitude). It will be three times smaller than the International Space Station (ISS)—a project involving around 15 countries (including the USA, Europe, Japan, and Russia). Its vocation is to conduct scientific activities. It should host non-Chinese scientists. It should help with the deployment of the future Xuntian telescope. This station is, as the Chinese government wishes, an essential factor of pride for the Chinese people, which shows that China is capable of challenging the USA. The repatriation of lunar samples is on the program and sending taikonauts to the moon is expected in 2036. The Chinese authorities also want to send a rover to Mars.

The Ambitions of the Chinese Space Program Are Military, But They Are Also Commercial

These large-scale operations increase China's international recognition, enhance the prestige of the state, and flatter Chinese pride. The conquest of space, however, does not only aim to strengthen international stature. Launching satellites has become a real business where China has a cost advantage over Ariane Espace. China has notably set up the Yaogan constellation, that is, around 30 reconnaissance satellites; these would have civilian objectives according to the Chinese authorities, but they are suspected of a military vocation by the West. The full implementation of the Beidou navigation program (Chinese GPS) was achieved in 2020. Rockets and satellites are manufactured by China Aerospace Science and Technology Corporation and by China Aerospace Science and Industry Corporation (150,000 employees cumulatively). And since 2014, private companies have been allowed to enter the business of manufacturing and launching satellites. If all these prestigious technological projects are synonymous with rebirth, they stand in stark contrast to the hundreds of millions of poor people in the country.

7.2 Electric-Powered and Driverless Cars

The Electric Car Sector, a Priority for the Chinese Authorities

China has strong ambitions with electric-powered cars. The country hopes to trigger with the electric car a "Kodak effect," that is, a technological revolution which would allow the redistribution of the cards in an established industry—the automobile industry—for the benefit of new players who would be Chinese. Yet, nothing is less certain because the combination of electric-powered car and batteries suffers from numerous faults (recharging time, range, weight, recycling, etc.). In the competition between the engines of the future, it is the battery-powered electric car that could play the role of fuse! Alternative technologies, like electric cars powered by hydrogen, have not said their last word.

From a Competitive Standpoint, the Electrical Car Sector Is in a Period of Fluidity

China has set itself the goal of having 3 million electric cars on its roads by 2025; as shown by Fig. 7.1, the bar was bypassed in 2020. Since 2015, more electric cars have been sold in China (3,500,000) than in the USA

(1,100,000). The milestone of 1 million sales of alternative propulsion vehicles was bypassed in 2018 thanks in part to subsidies granted to buyers by the government: 750,000 electric and 250,000 hybrids.

The market represented nearly 3.5% of sales in 2019 (834,000/ 23,529,000); the figure is even higher in the big cities. Chinese interest in electric vehicles waned, however, after the end of government subsidies in 2019. In 2020, despite the contraction of the automotive market that resulted from the Covid crisis, the electric segment continued to progress. In 2021, 3.3 million od electric cars were sold in China. The Chinese authorities for their part are committed to equipping charging stations: State Grid has equipped the 1200 km of motorway between Beijing and Shanghai. As early as in 2017, China had already developed a network of 200,000 charging stations. The government was able to increase the network to 4.8 million stations by 2020—more than the rest of the planet. It explores as well alternative formats like the swap of batteries. The future will tell whether the Chinese will take advantage of this major asset,

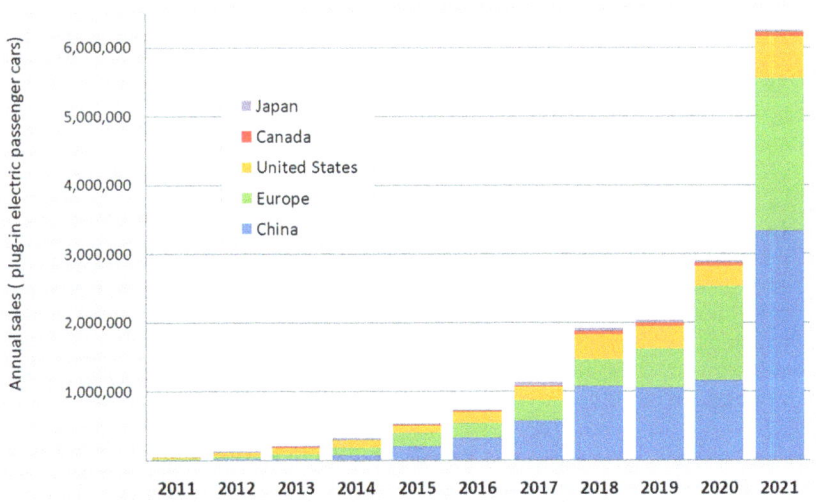

Fig. 7.1 Sales of plug-in electric passenger cars

especially regarding the potential to develop significantly beyond the boundaries of China which has not been the case until now.

The Electric Car Sector Contains Three Categories of Competitors

On one hand, there are traditional car manufacturers that have added electric vehicles to their catalog; these include SAIC, MG (ZS), BAIC, Wuling, Great Wall, and Geely with Volvo (Polestar) on the Chinese side, and BMW (iX3), Volkswagen (ID.), Nissan (Leaf) with foreign manufacturers. On the other hand, there are automakers focused on electrics. These are the two main players in the market—BYD and Tesla (see vignette below), but also a number of Chinese startups which want to emulate the success of Tesla.

> **Vignette: Tesla China—the First Wofe[1] in the Car Industry**
>
> In 2014, China opened up its market to electric car models to foreign manufacturers by reducing the advantages given to domestic models. Tesla, the brand launched by Elon Musk (the co-founder of PayPal and boss of Space X) was struggling to find its place in China. The CEO has managed to develop strong ties with the country. He signed an agreement with the authorities in 2018 to open a factory in Shanghai with an annual capacity of 500,000 vehicles—setting a precedent as it is the first foreign automaker to start a factory in China that it controls 100%. Tesla has invested $140 million to lease land in Shanghai over 50 years. And $2 billion to build the factory. This was built in record time—one year! This is the group's first factory outside the USA. Production of the Model 3 (its entry-level sedan) began in early 2020. It is expected to reach 250,000 vehicles per year. Production of the Model Y (its SUV) is expected to follow. Production in China allows Tesla to avoid prohibitive tariffs on imported cars. It also puts pressure on Chinese competitors. Tesla, which uses Panasonic batteries, has a competitive disadvantage with BYD because the Chinese company has its own batteries.

---

[1] Wholly Owned Foreign Enterprise.

As for the startups, two cases have to be mentioned: Faraday Future and Nio. Faraday Future was founded by Jia Yueting (49 years old in 2022). The Chinese billionaire made his fortune in internet video and smartphones. He posed himself as a rival to Tesla. He was to invest a billion dollars in a plant capable of producing electric vehicles in the USA in Nevada; but the project came to an end. His group Le Eco, founded in 2004, fell into turmoil in 2016, unable to pay its suppliers; in 2017, he quit the presidency of the conglomerate Le Eco. Another noteworthy case is Nio—supported by Tencent, Temasek, and Baidu. It was created in Shanghai in 2014, and has filed several thousand patents and developed several models (one crossover, and two SUVs) and in less than ten years. Its boss, William Li, was Entrepreneur of the Year in 2017. Production is contracted out to JAC. Like many companies in emerging sectors, electric car startups often flirt with bankruptcy (this was the case of Byton) as soon as the funds required for development are not there.

Finally, the third category is that of companies that have nothing to do with the automobile industry—but see the electric revolution as an opportunity. Thus, the Taiwanese Foxconn aims to become the Android of the electric vehicle industry; for this purpose, it offers an open software and hardware platform for an electric car. Even Huawei has embarked on the electric car. Presented at the Shanghai Motor Show in 2021, the sedan called Arcfox Alpha 5 will be produced by BAIC. Equipped with lithium-ion batteries, the car will initially be sold in China.

The Battery Industry Is Very Active

The battery business is dominated by three countries: South Korea, Japan, and China. Contemporary Amperex Technology Ltd. (CATL), based in Ningde (Fujian), founded by Zeng Yuqun and valued at $240 billion (at the end of 2021), is investing heavily. It is the world's largest producer of batteries for electric cars; it bypassed the South Korean LG in 2020. Shenzhen-listed, Chengdu-based battery producer Tianqi Lithium is pursuing a strategy of vertical integration upstream through the takeover or acquisition of stakes in lithium-producing companies; for example, it bought 24% of SQM—a Chilean lithium producer (Chile has half of the world's lithium reserves). It went public in Hong Kong in 2018. In 2016, Volkswagen signed an agreement for the development of electric vehicles with JAC (Jianghuai Automobile Co.)—the ninth largest Chinese manufacturer—based in Anhui. Volkswagen also joined in by buying a battery manufacturer (Guoxuan). BYD has some success with its blade batteries; Toyota became one of its customers for cars sold in China. Blade batteries exhibit an attractive low height and do not use cobalt.

The sector develops despite serious ecological threats such as the expected wave of used batteries to be recycled that will flood China in a few years. On top of this, the Chinese switch to the electric car is not necessarily associated with a better ecological environment since electricity is today produced by coal-fired power stations (we tend to forget, but electricity is not a source of energy, it is only a vector). China isn't just investing in electric cars. They have also invested in the hydrogen engine (fuel cell) for buses and trucks—movements largely supported by the authorities.

The Potential of Autonomous Vehicles

The Chinese government is seeking to take advantage of the emergence of autonomous vehicles—whether they are private cars, taxis, buses, or even trucks. In fact, there are conditions specific to the development of demand for autonomous vehicles in China; these new concepts can in particular help reduce urban traffic congestion caused by the booming Chinese automobile market and the resulting air pollution. Given its size, China could become the world's largest market. The relative novelty of the automobile, road infrastructure, and industry in China makes it easier to cope with the blurring of competitive boundaries between automakers, transportation companies, and big data mining platforms. China is seeking to set up, with national companies, the ecosystem required by autonomous vehicles: manufacturers of sensors, radars and cameras, platform developers, software designers, cartographers, storage companies, integrators, but also investors, lawyers, and more. Several startups have emerged such as Pony.ai, NavInfo, Neolix, or TuSimple. On the other hand, the weakness of the Chinese industry in semiconductors will work against the country if the driverless car is to develop.

7.3 The Block-Chain on the Government Agenda

One Additional Paradox

Fundamentally, the purpose of the "block-chain" is to strengthen digital trust between Internet players without going through a centralizing control authority. The certification of exchanges involves a set of data storage and sharing technologies where the execution of a transaction requires the consensus of all stakeholders. Technically, a chain of data blocks is fully replicated among the various network players. The paradox is that the centralized governance that prevails in China does not spontaneously mix well with this premise of decentralization! Yet, the authorities do not seem to be bothered and promote the development of block-chain technologies.

China Is Exploring Different Applications

Beyond cryptocurrencies (banned in China), applications include freight, logistics, health, and smart cities. Since 2016, the block-chain has been a priority investment set out in the thirteenth five-year plan (2016–2020). The subject is on the Chinese government's agenda and, as usual, rolled out in some advanced provinces (Shenzhen, Guangdong, and Jiangsu). The Standard Administration of China (SAC) is also at work. Several government agencies are leading projects in the fields of health, energy, surveillance, and cryptography. Not surprisingly, Baidu, Alibaba, Tencent, and JD.com are leading the dance in commercial applications. The block-chain is also exportable under the Belt & Road Initiative.

7.4 China and the Global Competition for Artificial Intelligence

The Competition Is Between China and the USA

Artificial intelligence (AI) is the new strategic horizon of the rivalry between the great powers (McKinsey Global Institute, 2017). It will impact automotive, finance, education, health care, pharmaceuticals, telecommunications, and manufacturing, among others. There are several countries that have AI strategies—the USA is the favorite, but China is not far behind and the European Union is in third place. India, Israel, and Australia are also in the race, but come after. This global competition is serious because the future leader of AI will have considerable power, will boost its economy, will create jobs, new businesses, attract investors, and revitalize other industries. AI is a priority for the Chinese government. It realized that China has an opportunity to assert itself as a leader in emerging technologies. AI is one of the pillars of the "Made in China 2025" plan (see Chap. 6) and China aims to be the world leader in artificial intelligence by 2030.

The USA is starting with an advantage thanks to its design capacity for semiconductors for AI systems. There would be 78,000 AI researchers in the USA in 2018 versus 39,000 in China—but the country could catch up. Chinese academics produce articles, and since 2020, China produces more papers than the USA (but US papers are more cited). Chinese researchers attend AI conferences. China also consistently files more AI patents than any other country—but most of those patents are filed by universities and public research institutes.[2] There are more and more funders (but, there is more private investment in the USA than in China). Chinese investors are entering the capital of young American AI startups. In short, the Chinese authorities are gradually gathering all the required ingredients (as highlighted in Chap. 3). And the government distributed the tasks to different stakeholders.

Chinese Economic Players

Baidu was given leadership in driverless cars, Tencent in medical, Alibaba in smart cities, and iFlyTek in voice interfaces. iFlyTek is one of the many dedicated startups created in China. It has already 700 million users. SenseTime, Megvii (with its flagship software Face ++), Yitu Technology, and Malong Technology are other examples in computer vision covering

---

[2] The open nature of AI science comes with fragile advantages as patents do not secure firms' positions.

facial, object, and image recognition. Megvii, created in Beijing in 2011, was valued at $4 billion at the end of 2019.

Many Internet companies have also embarked on the adventure of AI: Didi in ride-sharing,[3] Meituan in meal delivery, Toutiao in news aggregation, Metian in selfie beautification, Kuai Shou in live broadcasting, or even Deep-Blue in driverless buses. Even drone maker DJI uses AI. This is also the case with Meiya Pico Information, an IT security company specialized in digital data forensics. Based in Xiamen (Fujian), established in 1999, it employs more than 3000 people. It made the headlines in 2019 with its MF Socket mobile phone monitoring app. The picture also has to take into account military applications of AI; there is indeed a border, to say the least, porous between civilian and military applications.

Chinese AI Companies Start with at Least Four Advantages

First, the size of the country offers a fertile ground for the key success factor related to large AI databases. China has more Internet users (almost 1 billion) than the USA and Europe combined (312 and 390). The same goes for mobile phone users. And the Chinese people already use their mobile phones much more to pay for their purchases than the Americans. China accounted for 40% of global e-commerce. It has also become the world's leading robotics market (see Chap. 6). If there is an advantage in size somewhere, it is therefore probably more in the commercial field than in the military field.

Second, Chinese scientists are more and more numerous and active in AI, and the relative novelty of the field (compared to chemicals or cars, for example) makes it more likely to be innovative. In mature industries (like cars or chemicals), Chinese companies face foreign competitors which have been in the business for half or even one full century—quite hard to catch up and bypass!

---

[3] The largest ride-sharing company in the world is also the one with the largest databases.

Third, China is also a market eager for new developments. There is an appetite for financial applications (granting loans), voice and/or facial recognition (to buy a train ticket), distribution and assistance to decision-making like driverless cars, smart cities (under the umbrella of ZTE), and safe cities. The expected turnover is more than substantial.

Finally, the overwhelming support of the Chinese government and, a societal situation where private matters are ignored, work again in favor of Chinese companies—the concept of private data still has way to go in China. However, the Chinese authorities have started to think about a law to protect personal information inspired by the European General Data Protection Regulation (GDPR). On the other hand, China has a handicap in terms of hardware, and in particular semiconductor, limiting their computing capacities. The semiconductors they use for AI are not made in China—a lack which forces the Chinese companies to buy them from outside. Chinese supercomputers are thus equipped with processors from foreign suppliers (Americans and Malaysians, in particular).

The Export of Digital Authoritarianism and Other Dark Sides

The future of AI in China will have to contend with the disillusionments that often accompany high-tech: valuations that turn out to be far-fetched or business models that do not impose themselves. AI also poses the question of control over the data collected—could it be exploited by a government to repress opposition? The Chinese citizens, who adopted facial recognition without any problem in their daily life (to pay a bill at a restaurant, to buy a Sim card, etc.), are, for some of them, reluctant and ask to minimum supervision of practices when it comes to control. The scope of AI also raises questions. AI is thus used in China in facial recognition for mass surveillance—and especially of ethnic minorities in Xinjiang. Beyond the always possible technical errors, the model also suffers from discrimination bias.

China's experience in Xinjiang for the control of the Uighur population is now being sold to foreign countries. Chinese champion Hikvision equipped Johannesburg (South Africa) with facial recognition equipment. Yitu does business with Singapore. Other Chinese companies are present in Uganda, Mongolia, Zimbabwe, Myanmar, Kazakhstan, and Brazil. China has found the winning combo: it is targeting new export markets and it is at the same time promoting its model of population monitoring. The establishment of this system in countries where human rights are not a priority raises questions. Civil liberties in Africa are going to take a hit.

7.5 The Fintech

There is a strong vitality in technologies applied to finance (the so-called fintech), that is, technologies and innovations for the provision of financial services. These include mobile payment, internet banking, wealth management, credit scoring, P2P, insurance, and cryptocurrencies. These startups find themselves in competition with traditional financial institutions. The field grew strongly from 2000; it was not until the 2010s for the regulator to get involved.

Competitors are numerous. Chinese firms are quite active in the fintech sectors. Chinese companies have led the *Fintech 100* for several years with three in the top 10 and many startups in the top 100. The top 10 include Ant Financial, JD Digits, and Du Xiaoman Financial. Several subsets can be distinguished. First, there are the just mentioned Internet giants: Ant Group with Ali Pay, Tencent with WeChat Pay, and Du Xiaoman Financial (or Baidu Financial Services) among others. There are also insurers (like PingAn), software publishers (like Hundsun), startups (Jimu, Futus.com, etc.), but also banks (like ICBC), the Chinese supplier of payment cards (Union Pay), distributors (like JD Technology or Suning), and even manufacturers (like Haier).

The size of the market is a real amplifier—the widespread use of third-party payment is a good example (see vignette). The "indigenous innovation" regulation also forces foreign companies to locate their innovation on the Chinese territory if they want to continue to have access to the market. The benefits to be expected are numerous: reduction in labor costs, access to the local innovation systems, better adaptation to local needs and expectations, better response to standards and regulations, support from the Chinese government, promotion of company standards, and better interfacing with production. China must now demonstrate its capacity for innovation—not just incremental, but also disruptive.

Vignette: The Example of Payment Means

Everything is going fast in China. The Chinese consumers have skipped the home computer stage. Similarly, the Chinese consumers have also skipped the stage of the bank card, the use of which has remained marginal. They immediately embraced the smartphone. They have a large choice with Samsung, Apple, but also with many Chinese competitors like Huawei, Xiaomi, Oppo, Vivo, Lenovo, Gionee, Meizu, and others like Honor. All of them have recently entered this field of activity, each producing tens of millions of units. Xiaomi, for example, was created in 2010 and sold more than 100 million smartphones in 2018 (see Chap. 4). And the smartphone has invaded the lives of Chinese people much more than it has invaded the lives of Westerners. First, it is in numbers; China has reached 1 billion Internet users—97% of whom use mobile.

In everyday life, the use of smartphones has become widespread not only to listen to music, to watch a video, to order a taxi, but also to pay bills and expenses (metro, restaurants, groceries, a coffee at Starbucks, etc.), to rent a bike, to pay the rent, to send a "red envelope" during the holidays, and so on. There are of course limits: you cannot buy a Rolls Royce with your mobile. But, the limits in place are more than enough for the life of the middle class.

In 2010, cash was used for 99% of the transactions in China. Ten years later, the percentage went down to 41% (according to the 2020 McKinsey Global Payments Report).[4] Now you have to go shopping at Carrefour, Walmart, or Lotus to see the vast majority of customers—and not just young people, paying for their groceries in a second with their smartphone. Even in wet markets, most sellers and/or small producers display their QR code to receive payments. Several of my Chinese acquaintances have abandoned the use of cash for several years—and, they no longer even know where they left their wallet in their apartment (or they do not remember the last time they took cash out of an ATM). Let's get it right, this is not about payment by credit card, but about payment via electronic wallets. The practice of paying by smartphone has spread to college campuses where students pay for their expenses with their phones—even for a single Kwai.

Two options dominate: WeChat Pay and Alipay. The WeChat application (Weixin in Chinese) was launched in 2011 by Tencent. In 2018, WeChat bypassed the bar of one billion monthly active users and Tencent exceeded $500 billion in capitalization. In 2020, the number of monthly active users reached 1.2 billion—including 100 million outside of China. While WeChat is a social network that offers the WeChat Pay payment method, conversely, Alipay is a payment platform that has spread into social networks. Chinese consumers do not pay any fees to use WeChat Pay or Alipay (whereas you have to pay to have a bank card). These two technology companies, private,

(*continued*)

---

[4] This is Bad news for ATM manufacturers like Nixdorf, NCR, or Hitachi.

(continued)
carried out in a very short time a real take-over on the means of payment: Alipay took more than 50% and WeChat Pay nearly 40% of the $16 trillion of payments by mobile (according to Analysys). This might be a concern for the government, which sees this rise of private actors, but it is at the same time a means of controlling financial flows. It is perhaps to break this de facto duopoly that the Chinese government in 2019 granted PayPal the first license to a foreign firm to enter the payment market.

The wave is so powerful that it spills over the country's borders. The 28 million Chinese who visited Japan in 2018 convinced traders in the Land of the Rising Sun, whether in Ginza or elsewhere, to provide the Chinese visitors with the means of payment they are accustomed to and therefore offer them Alipay. The same goes for Russia. In 2018, Tencent launched its WeChat payment platform in Malaysia.

The paradigm is therefore different depending on whether you are in Europe or the USA or China. In Europe or in the USA, we have Apple Pay and Google Pay, among others, but few people use them. The West is blocked by the bank card that the system in place wants to continue to maintain. Contactless has long been in its infancy and is just starting to take off (with the exception of advanced countries like Sweden). In addition, Europe and the USA have lived through "uberization"; it was about attacking distribution players head-on. The stakes are exactly the opposite in China: companies like Alibaba, Tencent, and Baidu are looking to offer new channels to distributors. These Internet players are also making life easier for users by offering them an ever wider range of services. In return, users implicitly agree to let companies commercially exploit data that describes their behavior (analysis of the content of your emails, analysis of the content of your posted messages, analysis of the content of your requests on a search engine, etc.). And the actors of this revolution are accumulating an impressive amount of data on the purchasing behavior of the Chinese on an unprecedented scale. With a China which has now exceeded $10,000 in GDP per capita, we can see the weight of the movement. This example of the widespread use of smartphones shows how China can quickly meet high standards. It is up to foreign fintechs to reproduce the Chinese model in their country.

7.6 Conclusion

There exist several sectors where China demonstrates some technological advances. All those industries are born-global. Some are in pervasive sectors like the block-chain and artificial intelligence. Some others are more focused like the electric car, the driverless car, and the Fintech. We saw that they are—with the exception of space—relatively new industries. The future technological trajectory designed by the Chinese authorities has to be in emerging industries because in those industries China and other countries all start from scratch, and have to build new ecosystems (McKern et al., 2021). That's the advantage of targeting emerging industries rather than to try to establish positions in mature industries where ecosystems already exist (and take time to duplicate). The authorities still act as a conductor and continue to plan the development of those industries. Yet, the Chinese government entrusted to private companies the responsibility of developing those sectors; even the space industry started to open to private suppliers. One striking feature of the new industries (again, with the exception of space) is that the government permitted the creation of numerous startups. This competition allowed the best models to develop while weaker competitors disappear.

In summary, the aim of the Chinese authorities is to take advantage of emerging sectors. This is because of the attractive characteristics exhibited by those sectors: (a) all competitors started more or less from scratch, and more or less the same chances of success; (b) the ecosystem does not exist—it has to be built; (c) the rules of the industry have to be written, and it's tempting to compete to be the writer of those rules; (d) emerging sectors are not confined to incremental innovation; those environments are vivid for breakthrough innovation; (e) competitive fluidity is at its maximum, and all competitors can try with their own design to make it the future dominant design of the industry (Utterback, 1994).

References

McKern, B., Yip George, S., & Jolly, D. (2021). Innovation strategies of MNCs in China and their contribution to the national ecosystem. In F. Xiaolan, C. Jin, & B. McKern (Eds.), *Oxford handbook of China innovation* (pp. 397–414). Oxford University Press. isbn-13: 978-0190900533.

McKinsey Global Institute. (2017, April). *Artificial intelligence: Implications for China, discussion paper.*

Utterback, J. M. (1994). *Mastering the dynamics of innovation* (p. 253). Harvard Business School Press.

8

Seven Challenges

Abstract Seven challenges could impede the construction of technological advantages. Some shortcomings relate to domestic aspects, while others are on a global scale. In the first category, China will have to deal with quality issues, to create conditions for a real creativity so to produce breakthrough innovation (and not only incremental innovations), to increase the productivity of its economy, and not to fall into the middle-income trap. In the second category, I question the ability of China to set up global norms, to deal with societal issues raised by its negative externalities of its technological developments (like the Social credit system), or to sell technologies within the Belt and Road Initiative. None of these challenges is insurmountable, but domestic issues require to lift some cultural barriers, and global challenges require acceptance of countries China is dealing with.

Keywords Threats to development • Competitive advantage • Domestic challenges • Global challenges

The vision of success with technology creation promoted by Chinese authorities is counterbalanced by gray areas, and certain challenges must be overcome in order to succeed with their ambitious plans. These challenges could potentially impede the overall aim of becoming technologically self-reliant. I will cover the following seven shortcomings in this chapter:

- The lack of quality
- The default of creativity
- The productivity disadvantage
- The middle-income trap
- The impact on global norms
- The societal impact of technology
- The limits of the impressive "Belt and Road Initiative" (the new silk road)

8.1　Will China Solve Its Lack of Quality?

One Century Turmoil and Its Negative Impact on Quality

In history, "made in China" has meant a combination of craftsmanship, traditions, and attention to detail. Think of silk, ceramic, porcelain, lacquer, jade, bronze, wood, and the like. Chinese artisans have been working with jade since the Neolithic era! (jade cannot be sculpted, but it can be worked with an abrasive). Jingdezhen (Jiangxi) was the capital of porcelain in the seventeenth century. It took missionaries to spend some time there, recording the know-how to produce porcelain for a transfer of technology to take place from China to Europe. The collapse of the empire during the nineteenth century, wars, revolution, and communism destroyed this exceptional craft capital.

Since China's economic comeback over the past 40 years, the country has placed much more emphasis on quantity than quality. This is not a stereotype. Chinese manufactured products frequently suffer from a lack of quality—as it was the case after the war with everything that came from Japan.

Building construction suffers from the same flaws. There was no building that collapsed because the Chinese engineers calculate the structures of the buildings quite large (there was indeed a bridge that crashed due to poor workmanship, but this was explained by corruption—for which an official has been tried, sentenced to death, and executed). The faults relate more to finishing work and decoration: design errors, use of materials that are not resistant to the ravages of time, sloppy construction, and limited maintenance, among others. I remember a meeting at the work premises of an expatriate manager of a large European firm. The building where its offices are located is under construction. This is surprising because these premises seem new. He enlightens me on the why of these operations. The building was only built three years ago. And the floors of the ground floor collapsed: the builders had "forgotten" to tie the floors to the pillars of the building.

The challenge is known: unlike the German, Swiss, or Japanese engineer, who will let the product go out only if he is 99.9% certain, the Chinese engineer, under the pressure of his hierarchy, will be satisfied with 90 or 92%, even if it means making the required adjustments later—or even breaking everything and starting all over again; we know what this difference of 8 or 10% costs both in time and in resources (which thus gives the illusion that the Chinese are going faster than the others since the product is put on the market without having conducted in-depth tests).

Foreign Companies Acted as Quality Teachers

However, there are some circumscribed quality pockets, such as Lacoste polo shirts subcontracted in China or iPhones and iPads produced by Foxconn or Airbus A320s assembled in Tianjin or Mercedes cars produced in Beijing with Beijing Automotive Industry Corporation (BAIC).

Foreign companies came to China with their quality management methods. By working as an OEM for big foreign brands, a good number of Chinese companies have learned to make quality and have launched their own brands. Even more surprising, since the beginning of the 2000s, many Swiss watch manufacturers have not hesitated to source parts from suppliers in the Shenzhen region (imports from China to Switzerland in this area approached 1 billion Swiss francs). These examples prove that it is possible to make quality in China. But Chinese firms still have a lot to learn in this regard. There are also effective changes in several sectors: while critics from the automotive press looked with condescension to the crash tests of Chinese cars ten years ago, no one smiles now since there are Chinese cars (admittedly few) who obtain four or five stars—Qoros is one of these examples, even if its conception is not strictly Chinese since it is Sino-Israeli. As these quality practice islands (Lacoste, Foxconn, Airbus, Mercedes, etc.) diffuse in the Chinese manufacturing fabric, we will have to revise our judgment. Especially since an increasing number of Chinese consumers demand quality as illustrated by the success of German car manufacturers.

8.2 Will China Be Able to Boost Its Potential for Creativity?

Creativity is not the exclusive domain of the arts and culture, but it also affects the technological field and the economy. Recent economic history has shown that nations like Japan and South Korea, deemed uncreative in the 1970s, barely able to copy Western products, have since proven to be true creators of technology. This is very much the same path that China might had taken (Rein, 2014).

The Economic Landscape of China Has Changed Considerably

Several Chinese companies have already shown the way. This is the case with Alibaba, Baidu, or Tencent in the Internet (as shown in Chap. 5) and Huawei, Miui, Focus Media in information technology. The pattern is also true in more traditional industries with BYD (in automobile construction), Haier (in household equipment), Mindray (in operating theaters), or Sany (construction machinery and other heavy equipment).

Haier, for example, has designed a refrigerator with three compartments for the USA: a standard, a freezer, and an intermediate compartment which is made for ice-creams, of which Americans are heavy consumers. As an increasing number of Chinese companies have entered a process of internationalization, companies in developed countries are discovering that an increasing number of Chinese companies are not simply pursuing cost strategies: when the German company Putzmeister was taken over by Sany, it realized that the "Chinese Caterpillar" had a portfolio of more than 5000 patents.

Quantity or Quality?

China has recently taken the first place in several rankings: particularly in terms of the number of scientific publications, the number of patents filed, and the number of unicorns (as shown in Chaps. 2 and 3). As always in China, size blurs the perspective. Quantity is not necessarily the right measure because the question of quality remains. Creativity has so far been expressed more in business models than in scientific breakthrough or disruptive technologies. Thus, in the automotive, semiconductor, and pharmaceutical fields, Chinese groups have so far remained behind this worldwide race for innovation.

China Is Developing an Appetite for Startups

Chinese startups are now raising more funds than American ones. Financing in renminbi surpasses financing in dollars—with the exception of the Internet. Chinese startups provide a work environment that is second to none in Silicon Valley. Table 8.1 lists the top nine startups (as identified by Tracxn). The total number is difficult to assess, but it is for sure counted in millions. It could be that startup entrepreneurs may prefer to test new business models whose results may be observable more quickly than innovations based on basic research—with the exception of a few fields like quantum computing. And researchers don't care about basic research if they can quickly increase their standard of living significantly with a few operations closer to industry.

Table 8.1 Top nine startups in China

	Startup	Business	Creation
1	Ant Financial	Digital payment solutions for consumers and businesses	2014
2	WM Motors	Developer of AI-enabled electric cars	2015
3	Yuanfudao	Provider of online school-based test preparation platform	2012
4	Guazi	Online P2P marketplace for used cars	2012
5	Xingsheng Community Network Service	Provider of chain community for supermarket brand operator	2009
6	Suning Finance	Online platform for financial products	2015
7	Toutiao	Personalized news aggregator app	2012
8	Horizons Robotics	Provider of AI-enabled system-on-chips for the automotive industry	2015
9	Lufax	Online P2P lending platform for personal loans	2011

Source: https://tracxn.com/explore/Startups-in-China

Favorable Conditions for Creativity Exist

Is China ready for creativity? The country has some advantages. As creativity goes through experimentation, Chinese citizens have an advantage because they are first and foremost pragmatic. Creativity is about networking too—and at that level, they excel. One other advantage to China is a holistic mode of thinking which favors the understanding of complex and interrelated situations which frequently characterize innovation. Creativity is also about open-mindedness and curiosity—qualities that can be observed among Chinese people for foreigners who have traveled a bit in the country. The number of Chinese trained to be dreamy and skeptical is, however, small and concentrated in a few exceptional universities such as Peking or Tsinghua. In these more open contexts, creativity is more likely to be expressed. But creativity is also about questioning and observation—qualities that take time and are therefore difficult to develop in a society in a rush. Chinese people want everything, right away. The autocratic regime induced reflexes favoring short-term returns.

The First Obstacle to Taking Original Positions Is the Culture

Some traditional Chinese activities such as calligraphy show a cultural attachment to "doing better"; the gesture is repeated endlessly to improve it. Can these values that enhance learning hinder the search for "doing things differently"—a sine qua non of innovation? Creativity is also the criticism of dominant principles, it is to shake up established paradigms, provoke societal transformations, put mess, and so on. And this is precisely where it hurts, because nothing in their education prepares the Chinese citizens to these challenges. You have to see students perfectly lined up in schoolyards or engaged in calligraphy or learning written Chinese to grasp the weight of reproduction. In a society where censorship allows political power to protect itself, this censorship acts as a curb on the imagination and creativity of the Chinese people—unless, on the contrary, it acts as a stimulus to precisely circumvent it. And both bureaucracy and government interference asphyxiate creativity. The barriers to creativity are in the organization itself. Thus, ideological control is a reality in Chinese universities; and President Xi Jinping even wants to strengthen it. It is also in effect in private schools—more likely to promote Western content.

If we admit that innovation destabilizes the environment, we understand that innovation may have difficulty emerging in a society where, on the contrary, harmony and stability are sought. You have to be a madman, marginal, rebel, or, in any case, a little maverick to invent; just as many behaviors that are hardly popular in China. One could, however, retort that the Chinese citizens could let off steam and release their creative potential in one of the rare fields where adopting behaviors opposed to the dominant theses is authorized. Confrontation is not in Confucian culture. The fact remains that Confucian values, while they are a brake on creativity, do not necessarily prevent it. As evidenced by Japan, another society where Confucian values are strong, the country has produced a lot of innovations for half a century. You just have to wait for the master to disappear and make way for the disciple; the latter can then do whatever he wants.

8.3 Will China Overcome Its Productivity Disadvantage?

It is one of the Achilles' heels of China. Industrial processes mobilize armies of people. Factory tours show several hundred people all obediently and rhythmically performing the same sequence of a few seconds, repeated throughout the day. Productivity in the USA, Europe, or Japan—calculated as the ratio of the GDP to the number of hours worked in the country, is much higher than in China. OECD studies suggest that China has reduced the gap with the USA, but this gap is still substantial: productivity in China is 70–80% less (in manufacturing and in services). Many state enterprises and heavy industries are even in decline due to their low productivity. Chinese agriculture suffers from the same problems: farms are often too small; health controls are not always up to par and are not easy to regulate. With 40 million pig farmers, this activity also suffers from extreme fragmentation. This is why the Chinese authorities are seeking to inject more market there; the price of wheat, for example, was liberalized in 2016.

The race for productivity gains is, however, at the core of the strategy of companies like the Taiwanese FoxConn, which announced massive investments for increased robotization of its factories. The point was obviously well understood by politicians. Zhu Rongji, prime minister from 1998 to 2003, had already made it a line of action in the past. Along with automation, the government is also supporting digitization and upscaling as avenues for improving productivity. China has managed to gain productivity, but Western companies keep the advantage over Chinese companies; they can provide their Chinese subsidiaries with the technologies and methods that they have developed outside of China to remain competitive.

8.4 Will China Fall into the Middle-Income Trap?

These Countries That Escaped the Trap

Economists have shown that when a developing country reaches a certain level of per capita income (around 6000 euros per year), its growth goes from sustained (7–8%) to normal (1–3%). The locution "middle-income trap" is the one coined to describe emerging countries that have experienced very strong growth, but which were unable to transform their model and whose development stumbled on an average GDP per capita without ever joining the group of advanced economies (a per capita GDP of $12,500 is considered as the threshold for high-income countries). The World Bank found that out of 101 middle-income economies in 1960, only 13 had made it to the high-income group in 2008. The rising costs eroded the advantage that allowed their development and was not offset by a move upmarket and/or technological progress. Several Latin American countries have fallen into this trap: Chile, Mexico, Brazil, and Uruguay, in particular.

On the other hand, countries like Japan, Singapore, Taiwan, South Korea, and Poland have been able to avoid the trap. Starting from nothing in 1953 after a bloody civil war, South Korea, which was then a predominantly agricultural country,[1] now develops the best technologies, and has positioned several of its companies on a global level—Samsung and its 320,000 employees across 84 countries, but also LG, Hyundai, Kia, Hynix Semiconductors, and Hankook Tires, among others. It has raised the average income of its 50 million inhabitants to the level of European nations. Incidentally, South Korea trades twice as much with China as it does with the USA. Singapore, with significant investments in technology (electronics and pharmaceuticals, in particular), has transformed its economy. But, even though Singapore is ethnically Chinese,

---

[1] In the 1960s, the GDP per capita of South Korea was not very different from the one of Ivory Coast.

the size relationship with China has nothing to do with it (5.4 million people, including 1.3 million foreigners versus 1402 million according to the 2020 decennial census).

Will China Escape the Trap?

As the economy grows, Chinese wages go up, and the gap narrows with developed economies. China's cost advantage has eroded, and it costs now much more to produce in China than in Mexico or Vietnam. The Chinese nation wants to change the nature of its comparative advantage. Using Michael Porter diamond reference (Porter, 1990), China had lost its historical advantage based on low labor cost for the production of mass market goods; factor conditions have changed. But, the Chinese government has put in place related and supporting industries. China benefits also from a strong demand because of its huge domestic market. Figure 8.1 uses the four-step process described in Chap. 2 to show that the challenge is to switch from an advantage linked to low labor cost to an advantage based on innovation capabilities and advanced technologies. The question is whether China will be able to sustain growth like South Korea, Taiwan, or Singapore in terms of per capita GDP or if it will rather join the less happy trajectory of Brazil or Mexico? China is caught between the economies that remain competitive in terms of labor prices and the technologically advanced economies.

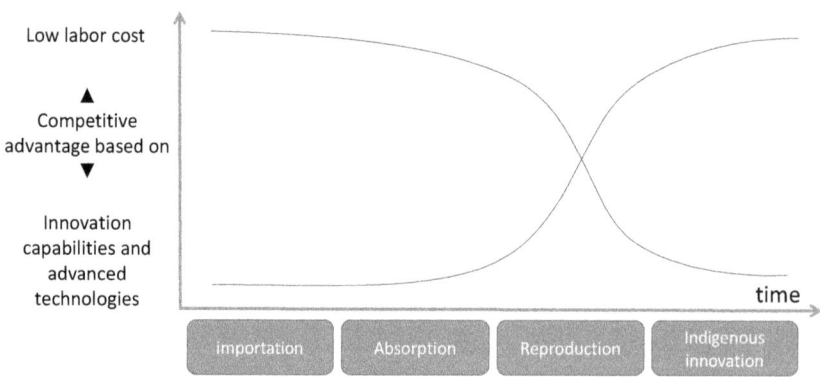

Fig. 8.1 The switch from cost to innovation

China has worked hard to transform its economy into higher value-added activities. Investments in R&D have not stopped growing to the point of becoming the second in the world with nearly $500 billion per year (see Chap. 3). China has developed the "Made in China 2025" plan to avoid falling into the trap; it invests in telecommunications, the Internet, artificial intelligence, facial recognition, and big data. However, these efforts are localized. Will they be enough to bring the countryside and the poor provinces out of their deprivation?

In China, everything is fine as long as you don't think per capita. Whenever a given data is compared to the size of the country, the comparison is not always flattering—starting with GDP per capita or imports per capita. In terms of per capita GDP, China is around $10,000, which positions it 75th in the world according to the IMF (well behind Poland, Chile, or Hong Kong SAR). Moreover, the per capita statistics are only an average which hide huge disparities. If China was to join the group of high-income countries and simultaneously remain communist, that would be a major conceptual change because all high-income countries are democratic countries today. This means that the Chinese economy would represent more than the combination of the USA and Europe: it would be a Copernican revolution, frankly a new world!

8.5   Will China Impact on Global Norms?

Setting standards in China follows a process different from the one existing in developed countries; government has the lead. China has been good at setting standards inside the country. The question is whether it will be able to push those standards at the global level?

The Standards Are Set by the Chinese State

In most developed countries, standard setting is done by the industry. It is the role of AINSI in the USA, BSI in the UK, Afnor in France, and Din in Germany, among others, that is, as many associations grouped together in a non-governmental umbrella organization, the International Organization for Standardization (ISO).

In contrast, in China, the setting of standards is the responsibility of the public authorities. The Ministry of Industry and Information Technology generates half of the standards. Several other ministries generate standards: there are the Ministry of Health for food safety, the Ministry of Transport for aviation, roads, and so on. However, companies are involved in the fixing process. Foreign companies can only participate in technical committees at best. Several government agencies are involved: such as Administration of Quality Supervision, Inspection and Quarantine (AQSIQ), and China National Institute of Standardization (CNIS). All of them operate under the supervision of the Standard Administration of China (SAC), which has been a member of the ISO since 1978.

China holds a record in the field; there are more than 150,000 standards (including 100,000 sectoral). The country produces a flow of 200–500 standards per month. Consequently, a large part of the industrial production is subject to standards. The setting of standards and the testing and certification procedures adopted can flirt with protectionism. These standards are barriers to foreigners entry on Chinese soil simply because of their complexity. The provinces have comparable powers with regard to the setting of standards vis-à-vis Beijing that European countries may have vis-à-vis Brussels.

China Is No Longer Just Looking for a National Impact, But for a Global Impact

Improving the international competitiveness of Chinese products no longer requires the adoption of foreign standards. The weight that China is taking in the global economy—through projects like the Belt and Road Initiative (BRI) or agreements like the Regional Comprehensive Economic Partnership (RCEP)—means that China finds itself able to influence future standards of activities that are emerging today, such as 5G, the Internet of Things, renewal energies, smart cities, autonomous vehicles, the exploitation of big data or quantum computing. Beijing's specific goal is to push its own standards globally, to move from rule-taker to rule-maker. That's the role of the plan entitled China Standards 2035 published during the summer of 2020. China wants first-class companies capable of doing standards, that is, connecting industries and markets worldwide. And the organizational centralization that prevails in China gives the country an advantage—especially when there is a need for coordination of multiple actors as, for example, in the case of smart cities.

If this capacity to set standards were to be expressed in these emerging fields, there is some concern for foreign countries. Indeed, we know well that mastery of data also means mastery of the system. In a completely different field, China is taking such a position in the production of lithium batteries that it should come as no surprise that in the future it will impose this standard on foreign car manufacturers.

8.6 Will China Deal with Societal Issues?

The emergence of China as a major actor in the economy and on the technology scene raises several societal issues that could impede its international development in the future. Technologies are not neutral. They come with what economists call externalities. They can be positive; for example, when a pharmaceutical company puts on the market a new drug, the benefit is not only for the company but for the society at large. On the opposite, externalities can be negative, that is, they can impact negatively the well-being of different stakeholders (and finally on shareholders as well).

A socially responsible company is a company that assumes its negative externalities such as the damage to which its employees may be victims, environmental pollution, unintended impacts of the product or service on the consumer, or decisions recognized as unethical. The socially responsible company recognizes the impacts of its activities and products on the well-being of its stakeholders and seeks to find ways to reduce these impacts. Depending on its social sensitivity, it will respond to pressures from its stakeholders or even get ahead of them. China certainly played an important role in securing the Paris climate agreement. But the externalities of industrial activity are well known: for instance, ecological disaster, health risks, archaic human resource management practices, and corruption. Therefore, the notion of corporate social responsibility is still not widespread in China. Safety standards in the industry are not necessarily a priority in the eyes of the hierarchy of manufacturing companies, as evidenced by industrial accidents. The low priority given to ethical issues even gives the Chinese firms an advantage in fields like genomics, tactile identification, or facial recognition.

Perceptions of externalities differ from one place to another. The Chinese Social Credit system is usually viewed negatively by the West, while it is very well accepted by Chinese citizens. The case is developed in the vignette below.

Vignette: The Chinese Social Credit System

China uses technology to control its citizens. The idea is not new: it was Qian Xueshen (the father of the Chinese ballistic missile program) who, from the 1990s, defended the idea of a system of social control generalized by artificial intelligence. The project was taken up in the 2000s by Lin Junyue. The "social credit" system was announced in 2014 by the Chinese government. It saw the possible applications of the Internet of Things, the richness of big data, and the power of artificial intelligence. This is the modern version of the personal file kept in the past by the managers of "danwei" (the work units that guaranteed work for life, housing, care, retirement, etc.). The system is under the supervision of the State Council, the National Development and Reform Commission, and the Central Bank. The authorities give it a civilizing mission: China wants to shape a new man. Social credit is presented as a tool for law enforcement; it's about differentiating good citizens from bad citizens based on whether or not they play by the rules. The system might also help to track down scammers, political dissidents, and possibly would-be terrorists.

How it works? The system involves measuring the reputation of each Chinese citizen through a score based on their driving behavior, the time they take to pay their bills, their defaults, their use of social networks, and more. The system is based on data collected on the Internet, but also on facial recognition systems coupled with camera networks deployed in the country (on the streets, buses, and public places). About 40 state agencies provide the administrative data to be compiled. Each Chinese citizen starts with a capital of 1000 points. Depending on his actions, he can lose or win points. Starting with a score set at A, the citizen can earn points and pass "AA" or even "AAA" or conversely lose points and go to "B," "C," or even "D."

Indiscipline at work, unpaid bills, and drunk driving, as well as criticism of the Chinese president on a social network, make the Chinese citizen lose points. The ones who erode their social capital run the risk of being

(continued)

(continued)
sanctioned: being at level B or C may prevent the approval of a loan. Sanctions can also be: the suspension of the access to a social network, the interdiction on staying in 4- or 5-star hotels, the restriction on transport (by train or by plane), the ban on leaving the territory, prevention of entry to university, prohibition of enrolling children in expensive private schools, exclusion of access to certain positions in state enterprises or certain professions, veto to receive state subsidies, to receive honorary titles, and so forth. After a test phase (notably in Hangzhou, Beijing, and Shandong), the system went operational for most of the provinces of China. There is the project of extending the system to companies (Chinese and foreign) that could be assessed according to their compliance with legal rules—by including, for example, the exceeding of polluting emission quotas. Behavior that does not comply with the law and regulations is blacklisted.

It is not the technology that worries so much, but the fear of being under surveillance and reducing the limits of privacy. The most deserving residents are honored. And the blacklists are public, searchable on the Internet. As always in China, the figures are astounding: there are tens of millions of people prevented from taking trains or planes. The Chinese call them the "laolai," the bad payers. There is no longer a place to hide in China whether you are a business or an individual. While we see this kind of system as a chimera, or as an Orwellian dystopia, the Chinese citizens see it more as a way to improve behavior. Many people are happy that those who smoke on trains or planes, who cheat or who do not pay their debts are blacklisted. In some respects, the evaluation of drivers and passengers of Uber or BlaBlaCar is also a rating system—except that it is not the State that manages, but service companies that we accept that they can block access.

8.7 Will China Overcome the Limits of the Belt and Road Initiative?

The Most Significant Chinese Geopolitical Initiative of Recent Decades

Everyone recollects the "Silk Roads" from their history lessons at school—and remembers that it resonated positively. It was out of a Western craze for silk, a refined fabric that only China then knew how to produce, that a major trade network was born. With silk, it was luxury that came from Asia. More broadly, it was a bridge between East and West that also served for the transfer of ideas and know-how—and also of religious beliefs. This was the time when raw silk bales were used as currency. There is, however, a less glamorous side of the Silk Roads such as the spread of the Black Death. This had come in the fourteenth century to Europe and Africa from the Eurasian steppes; Europe lost one-third of its population (25 million out of 75).

The concept of "New Silk Roads" was skillfully developed by President Xi Jinping in 2013 (one year after taking office) in Astana during a visit to Kazakhstan. Although the announcement went then almost unnoticed, the theme has since become the centerpiece of President Xi's foreign policy and international economic strategy. The geopolitical message is strong: it is about connecting South Asia to Europe via Central Asia, that is, facilitating economic cooperation with other regions and countries. Rail and pipelines replace caravans and camels. HP computers and beach buoys replace silk fabrics and spices.

The keyword is "connectivity"—connectivity between East and West, but also at the level of all intermediate segments at the regional level. An axis leaves from Chongqing, crosses Xinjiang, and joins Europe via Russia or Iran, and then Turkey. China wants to develop and secure sea routes to the Middle East and Europe. From the South China Sea to the Indian Ocean, East Africa, the Red Sea, and the Mediterranean Sea. In fact, sea transportation is much less expensive than land transportation. The now so-called Belt and Road Initiative (BRI) covers multiple objectives: economic, financial, geopolitical, military, cultural, and also image.

One Trillion-Euro Initiative

BRI is a colossal project, unparalleled in the history of mankind. This initiative takes shape through trade agreements, investments in transport networks (roads, railways, ports, oil pipelines, gas pipelines), and financial support structures—all means of investing abroad the extraordinary Chinese foreign exchange reserves (over 3 trillion) rather than in US treasury bills. These are impressive bets considering that a pipeline is there for a few decades, but at the same time, the tap can be turned off overnight. The construction of 30 nuclear power plants is on the program in the countries concerned. China is using the BRI to penetrate as far as the Balkans (Albania, Bosnia and Herzegovina, North Macedonia, Montenegro, and Serbia)—notably with infrastructure projects. The road is not only land and sea but also digital.

The Digital Component

China has opened a door to exportation of all its new technologies through the BRI; the new silk roads are not only on earth and on the sea, there is also a digital road fostering connectivity. One of the components is the construction of a communications network with its batch of optical fiber cables, international submarine cables, satellites, and other related equipment. More than a road, it is a network. Telecommunications networks, internet connections, the Beidou satellite navigation system (the Chinese GPS), cloud computing, IOT, railways digital infrastructures, logistic automation, enterprise resources planning are applications desired by all countries on the new silk roads. There are also plans to establish science parks in several of those countries.

The Dominant Chinese Interests

The operation responds to a real need for logistics and energy infrastructure in the targeted countries. But it should primarily benefit Chinese companies that manufacture high-speed trains, port cranes, telephone equipment, and so on. And Chinese-made trucks, excavators, cranes, and jackhammers are used to build this infrastructure. The BRI is an encouragement to Chinese companies to go international. These are all opportunities to deal with Chinese overcapacity.

The Chinese "political" banks, that is, the China Development Bank (CDB) and the Export-Import Bank of China (EIBC)—but also commercial banks like the CCB, the ICBC, and the BOC—finance the projects. There is also the Silk Road Fund created in 2014 with $40 billion in capital. The new Asian Infrastructure Investment Bank (AIIB), created also in 2014, and its 100 billion initial endowment may also be responsible for financing these projects. The Chinese authorities often make obtaining loans conditional on Chinese contractors. US and European companies are not well placed to conquer part of these infrastructure markets.

The Growing Oppositions

The oppositions come from foreign countries—especially Europeans, who believe that China does not sufficiently open the door to tenders and that it is mainly Chinese companies that are the beneficiaries. In fact, a study by the Center for Strategic and International Studies (CSIS), published in 2018, revealed that 89% of contracts go to Chinese companies. As a result, countries like the UK are dragging their feet to join the BRI.

The oppositions also come from countries closer geographically which are not comfortable with the rise in power of China. Malaysia, for example, suspended several Chinese projects (a rail link and two pipelines) after Mahathir returned to power; the price of the high-speed line was finally revised downwards. The Pakistani government also expressed the wish in 2018 to revise the past contracts. While investment in infrastructure (ports, pipelines, railways, etc.) must support economic development, countries are struggling to get a return on their investments and are therefore harassed to repay their loans. Sri Lanka failed to amortize the port of Hambantota, to the extent that control of it has been ceded to the Chinese contractors for 99 years and Sri Lanka has therefore moved into the Chinese sphere of influence. The Maldives has also fallen into the debt trap and is asking for it to be postponed. Pakistan could also find itself in default of payment. The same question is asked for many other countries: Mongolia, Montenegro, Laos, Djibouti, Kyrgyzstan, and Tajikistan. China's debt policy is becoming an instrument of political influence.

This is the return of the "unequal treaties," except that this time it is China which initiated them. The BRI also entails a risk of asymmetry if the flows on those roads are unbalanced. Beyond these competitive aspects, the ecological heritage of the BRI has so far aroused little opposition. Yet these new Silk Roads are a frontal attack on the Paris Agreement (COP 21). This logistics development is a societal misunderstanding at a time when the keyword is the relocation of industrial sites close to places of consumption. The ecological damage is immediate when it comes to the construction of infrastructure.

8.8 Conclusion

China invested billions into technological development. Yet, this chapter has shown that several aspects could impede the construction of a competitive advantage based on innovative capabilities and advanced technologies. Those fragilities are real. Failures in several of those aspects at the same time might stick China into a difficult position.

There are potential solutions for the question marks raised in this chapter. For example, the question about creativity can be solved as soon as companies and society create the conditions for creativity. But, I wonder whether the government will or not support this change?

References

Porter, M. E. (1990). *The competitive advantage of nations* (p. 885). The Free Press.
Rein, S. (2014). *The end of copycat China: The rise of creativity, innovation, and individualism in Asia* (p. 248). Wiley.

9

The Conductor and Its Disciplined Performers

Abstract China strongly invests in technology, takes advantage of a massive market, and benefits from a stable political regime—all three aspects contributing to the success of its national system of innovation. The State and the Communist Party play a definitive role: authorities are like a conductor, and actors cannot depart from the partition. Technological goals are nevertheless impacted by political factors and the future of China is heavily dependent on the evolution of its relationship with the USA. Indigenous innovation is mostly incremental, but some breakthrough innovation might come from emerging areas.

Keywords Conductor • Performer • Incremental innovation • Breakthrough innovation

This book has shown that China followed, at a much larger scale, the South Korean path of technological development. In this sense, the Chinese case is not unique. Yet, this development came with some specific Chinese characteristics. This includes:

- A massive market demand
- An overwhelming role played by the government and the consequential need to build political connections
- A dependence on foreign technologies
- An inclination for incremental innovation

In summary, the success of China is a combination of technological investment, market conditions, and political environment. China has undoubtedly accumulated resources for fostering innovation and developing advanced technologies. Yet, one question still remains: will the country be able to transition from quantitative accumulation to a qualitative leap forward? Some examples, like quantum computing and communication, seem to open up this possibility. But, this type of move will be hard to achieve in mature sectors where established western companies have been leading for a long time.

Chinese companies take advantage of a gigantic market. Market size acts as an amplifier. And, massive market size is an advantage not only because of this huge demand but because, on the supply side, it allows the creation of numerous startups. Market competition amongst those startups helps the best models to emerge, while the weak disappear.

One interesting conclusion of this book is that the pursuit of technological goals cannot solely be explained by technical criteria. The key feature of the Chinese case is the impact of politics—inside—but also outside the country. As illustrated by 5G, the refusal of the USA is first explained by political factors. The arrest of the daughter of Huawei founder is conversely a political move to counter the technology company. Similarly, the decision to stop supplying important Chinese buyers with US semiconductors is as well motivated by politics. Technology decisions are not made in a vacuum.

President Xi came to Davos (in 2017) to reaffirm that China favors market economy. Yet, this book makes clear that technology creation is a process deeply under the control of the State forces. The Chinese authorities are the conductor. All the stakeholders of the Chinese national system of innovation are interpreting. Metaphorically, I would say they are expected to follow the same musical partition, I mean the different existing governmental plans: five-year plan, Made in China 2025, China standard 2035, … and they cannot reinterpret the melody, they have limited space for creating new lines. And if the performers want to play a song which is not aligned with the expectations of the conductor, they will be sanctioned, as Jack Ma and others have been. It does not mean that there is no vitality. As mentioned before, in emerging industries, government favors the emergence of startups, and that market mechanism helps promote the best models and eliminates the weakest. So, the market economy is present in new sectors.

China has accomplished an impressive trajectory. And the success can be attributed to the political forces which orchestrated the development. Yet, those forces which created the success might also generate failure in the future. As such, the recent trend for national self-reliance might negatively impact future technological developments.

Index[1]

A
Absorption capabilities, 9, 11
Acquisitions, 13, 16–19, 23
Advanced countries, 8, 20, 27
Alibaba, 76–85, 88, 90–92
Alipay, 80, 84
Alliance, 15
Apple, 66, 68–70
Applied research, 3
Artificial intelligence (AI), 112, 119–123, 125
Assimilation, 8, 10, 12
Automation, 107–108

B
Baidu, 76, 77, 84–86, 91, 92
BATX, 76–78, 95

Belt & Road Initiative (BRI), 128, 138, 141–145
Block-chain, 112, 119, 125
Breakthrough, 23–24
BYD, 116, 118
ByteDance, 84, 89, 93, 95

C
Catch-up, 9, 21–22
China Academy of Sciences, 30
China Mobile, 60, 63, 71–72
China Railway, 103
Chinese authorities, 64
Chinese communist party, 62, 63, 69
Chinese government, 60, 63, 64
Competition, 60, 66
Concentrated, 60, 71

---

[1] Note: Page numbers followed by 'n' refer to notes.

Conductor, 56
Confucianism, 30
Connections with authorities, 5
Creativity, 128, 130–133, 145

D

Deng Xiaoping, 2, 9–10
Dependence, 23
Diaspora, 13–15, 19
Didi, 76, 89, 91–92, 95
Digestion, 102–104, 109
Diversification, 79, 81–82,
  85–86, 88–89,
  92, 94
Driverless cars, 112, 114–118, 120,
  122, 126

E

Ecosystem, 67, 71
Education system, 30–37
Electric cars, 114–118, 126
Ele.me, 82, 89–92
End of development, 3
Endogamy, 13
Exogamy, 11, 13

F

Fintech, 8
5G, 63–67, 71
Foreign companies, 2, 5, 10,
  12–14, 20
Foreign technologies, 8, 15–19
Fundamental research, 3

G

GAFAM, 76, 78, 94
Gaokao, 32
Geely, 16–18
Google, 76, 79, 84–86, 90, 93
Guanxi, 12

H

High-tech startups, 30
Huawei, 60–68, 70, 71

I

Indigenous innovation, 8, 19–24, 26
Infrastructures, 30, 41
International development, 98–109

J

Jingdong, 90
Joint-ventures, 9–13, 15, 23

K

Knowledge, 8, 10, 13, 14, 16, 27

L

Lei Jun, 67–70

M

Ma Yun, 78
Mao Zedong, 2
Massive market, 72

Mature industries, 21
Meituan, 89–92
Middle-income, 106

N
National champions, 106
National system of innovation, 29–56
Nuclear industry, 104, 105

O
One billion, 77, 84, 87, 92

P
Patents applications, 9, 26, 27
Performer, 56
Photovoltaic panels, 98, 100, 101, 109
Pinduoduo, 89, 90
Primary development, 3
Productivity, 128, 134
Public policy, 7–28

Q
Quality, 128–132
Quantum, 24

R
Rare earth, 98–100, 109
Regulatory framework, 30, 54–55
Ren Zhengfei, 62–65
Reproduction, 15–19
Research universities, 30, 33, 34, 53
Returnees, 13, 14

S
Samsung, 62, 66–68, 70
Scale effects, 5
Sciences & technology parks, 39–42, 44, 55
Scientific articles, 24, 25
Shareholder, 88, 89, 91
Shenzhen, 30, 38–42, 45, 48, 54
Social credit system, 140–145
South Korea, 8, 23
Space industry, 2
Suntech, 101, 102
Suzhou, 53

T
Takeover, 16–18, 23
Teaching universities, 33
Technological autonomy, 19
Technological learning, 10–12
Technology transfers, 2
Tencent, 76, 77, 81, 85, 87–91
Tesla, 116, 117
TikTok, 89, 93
Trajectory, 8

U
Unicorns, 30, 42–44, 55
US authorities, 63, 65

V
Value-chain, 98, 108

W
WeChat, 84, 87

X
Xiaomi, 60, 67–71

Y
Yihaodian, 89, 90

Z
Zhangjiang, 42
Zhejiang, 78, 78n2
Zhongguancun, 40, 42
ZTE, 62, 64, 65, 68, 71

GPSR Compliance
The European Union's (EU) General Product Safety Regulation (GPSR) is a set of rules that requires consumer products to be safe and our obligations to ensure this.

If you have any concerns about our products, you can contact us on

ProductSafety@springernature.com

In case Publisher is established outside the EU, the EU authorized representative is:

Springer Nature Customer Service Center GmbH
Europaplatz 3
69115 Heidelberg, Germany

www.ingramcontent.com/pod-product-compliance
Ingram Content Group UK Ltd.
Pitfield, Milton Keynes, MK11 3LW, UK
UKHW021251180426

11946UKWH00004B/73